TQ

120A

TO 120A

BLACKABY

BROADMAN
& HOLMAN
PUBLISHERS

NASHVILLE, TENNESSEE

TQ120A

ISBN 13: 978-0-8054-3068-4

ISBN 10: 0-8054-3068-7

Broadman & Holman Publishers

Nashville, Tennessee

www.broadmanholman.com

Unless otherwise noted, all Scripture quotations have been taken from the *Holman Christian Standard Bible*® Copyright © 1999, 2000, 2002, 2003 by Holman Bible Publishers.

Dewey Decimal Classification: 242

DEVOTIONAL LITERATURE

Printed in the United States of America

1 2 3 4 08 07 06 05

TABLE OF CONTENTS

INTRODUCTION

Could there be anything more exciting than to wake up each morning, knowing you're going to meet with God? How incredible to think that you can talk directly with the Creator of the universe, telling him your problems and listening to what he has to say about them!

Yet that's exactly what you can do each day, because God invites you to spend time with him! You are free to tell him whatever is on your heart. You can ask him any question and find comfort from any pain. God promises to respond to you with love. This makes meeting with God something you ought to look forward to each day with tremendous anticipation.

This *TQ120* devotional book is meant to assist you as you meet daily with God. It assumes you already have a personal relationship with him through faith in Jesus Christ. If you do not, you can begin a relationship with him by praying and asking God to forgive you of your sin. Then commit yourself to doing whatever he tells you.

This devotional book has Scripture verses that will introduce you to wonderful promises from God that can change your life. As you read the devotions, be sure to have your Bible with you, because although we've done our best to make our words valuable, God's Word to you is vital!

Also, keep a pen with you so you can write your thoughts in the journaling sections—because when the Lord of the universe says something to you, it's important enough to write down! Later, you can look back over the things God has said to you during your times with him and see how he has been leading you, day by day. This will make this book a great source of comfort to you as you see how God has been guiding you and sharing his love with you.

Commit yourself to spending regular time with God each day. It will change your life!

JESUS TALKING

WHAT WORDS COME TO MIND WHEN YOU THINK ABOUT WHAT GOD IS LIKE?

AWESOME? ALMIGHTY? FAITHFUL?
LOVING? PURE? HOLY?

What about just the word "Jesus"? When God the Father wanted to show us exactly what he was like, what did he do? He sent his Son, Jesus. That's why when people looked at Jesus, they were seeing what God was like.

And that's why when you read Jesus' words in the Bible today, you're hearing the wisdom of God . . . right here, right now.

Have you ever had a favorite teacher, someone who impacted your life in a significant way? Perhaps that person set an example for you that challenged you to strive for excellence. Maybe he encouraged you when you were struggling and gave you special care and attention. Maybe she inspired you by simply believing in you. A good teacher can touch your life in ways that will last forever.

Jesus was a teacher like that. But he was more than a good teacher. He was God. Every word he spoke was backed by a life of total obedience to his Father. Every instruction he shared was given in unconditional love. When he spoke about holy living, he not only knew what he was talking about, but he was actually able to make his disciples holy.

Even the best teachers can make mistakes . . . but not Jesus. The things he said will always be true. So as you read these first ten devotions, be aware that you're learning not just from a great teacher but from the holy Son of God. Jesus can teach you today just as effectively as he taught his disciples two thousand years ago. Be prepared to learn things from the Master Teacher that will forever change your life!

HEY, NO FAIR!

READ AHEAD: LUKE 12:42–48

Even more will be expected of the one who has been entrusted with more. Luke 12:48

From the time we're very young, most of us spend a lot of energy making sure that everything's fair. We watch our parents to make sure they don't give our brothers or sisters more than they give us. As we grow, we watch our friends to make sure they don't have better stuff or nicer clothes or better-looking dates than we do.

We do the same thing with God, too. When we see how he blesses someone else—with talents or brains or naturally curly hair—we just can't resist the urge to compare it with what he's given us.

Is that really the issue, though? Is this some kind of contest to see who gets the most? The Bible leaves no question that God is completely fair. So our problem can't be that God has shortchanged us.

Jesus made it clear that we're not responsible for what he gives others but for what he gives us. So if any unfairness is involved, it's usually in the way we mishandle what God entrusts to us. Maybe we just haven't done much with what we've been given.

Take some time to consider how well you're handling your blessings. The important thing in life is not who gets what, but how well you manage what you get. As a Christian, you've received a lot, so be ready to give an account for what you've done with it.

WHAT COULD YOU DO TO START SQUEEZING EVERY DROP OUT OF THE GIFTS GOD HAS GIVEN YOU?

READ UP: MATTHEW 20:1–15 • LUKE 16:10–13

WHAT DO YOU SAY?

READ AHEAD: LUKE 9:18–20

"But you," He asked them, "who do you say that I am?" Peter answered, "God's Messiah." Luke 9:20

Jesus had spent three years teaching his disciples. It was time to see if they'd learned what he wanted them to know.

For three years they'd watched his life. They'd seen him perform miracles, cast out demons, heal disease, and raise the dead. They'd marveled at his wisdom. They'd seen him escape the cunning traps of the Pharisees. They'd seen him live in private all that he professed in public—a pure, holy, and victorious life.

Now Jesus wanted to know what conclusions they had drawn. First, he asked a leading question (verse 18): "Who do the crowds say that I am?" The disciples had heard all sorts of theories from others about who Jesus was. After they had mentioned a few of them (verse 19), Jesus asked his second, more poignant question: "But you . . . who do you say that I am?"

Everyone has an opinion about Jesus. People say he was a great teacher, a moral man, a left-wing radical, or a fictional character who lived only in first-century literature. But whatever others think about who Jesus is—or was—is not the most important question. The ultimate question is: "Who do you say that he is?"

If you've been hiding behind the opinions or the faith of others, it's time to step out and declare for yourself who Jesus is: the Christ, the Son of the living God. Are you ready with your answer?

WHAT MAKES YOUR OPINION OF CHRIST ANY MORE VALID THAN SOMEONE ELSE'S?

READ UP: JOHN 1:43–51 • JOHN 6:66–69

AN EYE ON YOURSELF

READ AHEAD: LUKE 6:37–42

First take the log out of your own eye, and then you will see clearly to take out the speck in your brother's eye. Luke 6:42

Most of us live by a double standard. We judge ourselves one way, but we use a different set of rules for others. When we sin, we're quick to explain the reasons behind our disobedience:

- "I was exhausted."
- "I didn't know what I was doing."
- "I was under a lot of stress."

When it comes to other people, however, that's another case. We put on our judge's robes and pronounce them guilty, regardless of the evidence:

- "He knew better."
- "This isn't the first time she's done this."
- "There's just no excuse for that!"

It's good to help your friends live the life God desires, but your first priority should be to make sure your own life is pleasing to God. When you're diligent to keep sin out of your own heart, you'll then be able to see others in the correct perspective.

Whenever you're involved in willful, deliberate sin, it distorts everything you see. But when your heart is pure, you won't be so quick to condemn others for their sins, nor will you jump to conclusions about them. You'll have the grace to help without judging.

WHAT MAKES US SO COMFORTABLE WITH OUR OWN SINS, YET SO IRRITATED BY THE SINS OF OTHERS?

READ UP: ROMANS 14:10–12 • JAMES 1:22–25

TIME TO PRAY

READ AHEAD: LUKE 5:12–16

Yet He often withdrew to deserted places and prayed. Luke 5:16

People were always trying to figure out where Jesus' power came from. Some attributed it to the work of Satan. Others explained his miracles away as illusions.

Jesus, however, made no secret about the fact that his power came from his Father. That's why it was so vital for Jesus to spend lots of time in prayer, seeking his Father's will.

Many of us have difficulty spending time alone with God. I mean, how do we cram one more thing into our already packed days? We lead such busy lives. We have so many demands on our time. It's not always easy to find a private time or place, even at home. There are just so many other things to do . . . in between phone rings.

But take a closer look at Jesus. It wasn't as though he had lots of extra time on his hands. Jesus was an extremely busy man! And when the news began to spread that he could heal the sick and feed the hungry, the less and less privacy he had. Everywhere he went, the crowds followed.

That's why in order to spend time with his Father, he had to get up unusually early and sneak away from the crowds to find a quiet place.

If Jesus, the Son of God, needed time with his Father in order to live the victorious Christian life, why would we ever think we could do it alone?

WHY DO WE TEND TO PREFER NOISE AND ACTIVITY OVER QUIETNESS AND STILLNESS?

READ UP: LAMENTATIONS 3:22–27 • REVELATION 8:1–4

6

SAY IT LIKE YOU MEAN IT

READ AHEAD: LUKE 6:46–49

Why do you call Me "Lord, Lord," and don't do the things I say?
Luke 6:46

Many would-be disciples followed Jesus while he walked throughout the countryside. They listened to him teach, but they rarely if ever did what he said. Even so, these pretenders boldly called Jesus their Lord, the same way his true disciples did.

Jesus confronted them for this, exposing the hypocrisy of letting the word "Lord" roll so easily off their tongues while their lives remained unchanged. They were calling Jesus their Master, yet they refused to be his servants. They sacrificed nothing for him. They continued to pursue their own goals. They carried on with whatever lifestyle suited them.

Yes, they had changed their vocabulary, but not their values.

Jesus wasn't conned by their show of loyalty. He likened them to a fool who built a house on sand without taking the time to lay a solid foundation. At first, the house looked the same as the wise man's house, which had been carefully laid on a solid rock. But when the winds and the rains came, the fool's house collapsed into a pile of rubble while the wise man's house stood firm.

Are you a wanna-be disciple? Do you say words you think Jesus wants to hear but refuse to do what he asks you to do? Perhaps you've been around genuine disciples enough that you've adopted their vocabulary without making Jesus your Lord.

Jesus wants you to have much more than Christian vocabulary. He wants you to have his new kind of life.

IS IT BEING JUDGMENTAL TO EXPECT PURE, HOLY LIVES FROM PEOPLE WHO PROFESS CHRISTIANITY?

READ UP: ISAIAH 58:3–14 • MATTHEW 16:24–25

TIME WILL TELL

READ AHEAD: LUKE 7:31–35

Wisdom is vindicated by all her children. Luke 7:35

At times, it seems like you just can't win. No matter what you do, someone is always there to point out how wrong you are.

For example, people criticized John the Baptist for being different. He didn't fit in. He dressed weird. He ate bugs. So his detractors concluded he must be demon possessed.

Jesus, on the other hand, dressed and ate as others did. But guess what? Those same critics found fault with him because he fit in *too well*, because he wasn't different *enough!* They observed him spending time in the homes of those they considered riffraff, so they considered him a glutton and a drunkard—hardly *God* material!

Two lessons to be learned here:

(1) *Be careful before condemning.* Jesus' critics looked down on everyone who didn't live exactly like they did. We should allow others to follow Christ's leading, not rejecting or accusing them just because God's plan for them isn't identical to his will for us.

(2) *You can't please everybody.* When you know what God wants you to do, don't let others' criticism deter you from doing what's right. In trying to please one group of people, you'll just end up offending another. Instead, base your life on God's Word, do exactly what he tells you to do, and let time vindicate your choices.

HOW CAN YOU TELL WHETHER OR NOT GOD APPROVES OF THE DECISIONS YOU'RE MAKING?

READ UP: MATTHEW 10:16–25 • 1 THESSALONIANS 4:1–8

SURE ABOUT THAT?

READ AHEAD: MATTHEW 3:13–17

There came a voice from heaven: "This is My beloved Son. I take delight in Him!" Matthew 3:17

Can you imagine what must have gone through John the Baptist's mind when Jesus asked to be baptized by him? The situation just seemed backwards to John.

But Jesus had a Word from his Father that he should be baptized—and that his cousin John should do it. So both men did as God said. As a result, the crowds heard the audible voice of the Father, voicing his approval for his Son!

Sometimes God will ask you to do something that doesn't seem to make sense. You'll have another plan in your head that you think is more reasonable. It's far more important, though, for you to obey God than to go with your own reasoning. In your effort to follow your own best thinking, you can actually disobey him.

This can happen in many ways. Perhaps God has called you to be a missionary, but you've always been a homebody. You don't think you're cut out for life in a foreign country. Maybe you have your career all planned out, but God tells you to go to seminary. Whatever it is that God tells you to do, don't try to convince him that he's got you pegged wrong. Just do it.

When you do what God asks, regardless of whether it makes sense to you, you'll experience his approval. No other achievement will ever match the joy of hearing your Father say he is pleased with you!

WHAT ARE YOUR USUAL EXCUSES FOR NOT DOING WHAT GOD TELLS YOU TO DO?

READ UP: 2 KINGS 5:1–14 • LUKE 12:54–56

HURRY HOME

READ AHEAD: LUKE 15:11–32

While the son was still a long way off, his father saw him and was filled with compassion. Luke 15:20

Jesus told the story of an arrogant young man who made a series of selfish choices which brought humiliation to his family and suffering to himself. But when he finally came to his senses, he felt like he could never undo the damage he'd done. He'd gone way too far. There was no hope of going back to the way things were before.

Have you ever felt that way? Have you ever woken up and realized you'd made a terrible mess? You'd blown it so badly, the last thing you wanted to do was to face God, let alone ask his forgiveness. You were sure you'd never again enjoy the closeness with him you once knew.

But even while this son was sinning his way to rock bottom, his father was watching for him, waiting to welcome him home. He wasn't sitting at home planning how to punish his worthless boy—if he ever dared show up! No, this father was longing to see his son's face again. He was planning the celebration party he'd throw for him if his son would just come home.

When the day finally came and he recognized his son's silhouette on the horizon, the father took off at a run—filled with joy, not judgment!

Jesus, of course, was describing your heavenly Father. So if you're a prodigal, don't waste another day avoiding God. Just go home. He'll be there. Running to meet you.

HOW CAN GOD DEMAND OBEDIENCE YET FORGIVE SIN AT THE SAME TIME?

READ UP: JOHN 8:2–11 • ROMANS 8:1–4

THANKS ... REALLY

READ AHEAD: LUKE 17:11–19

He fell down at His feet, thanking Him. And he was a Samaritan.
Luke 17:16

Don't you just love Luke's little postscript here—"And he was a Samaritan"? We know from Jesus' story of the "Good Samaritan" that Jewish people despised this ethnic group. They were considered low-lifes, the dregs of society.

It's interesting that Jesus chose a Samaritan, then, as the hero in his story. Here were ten men, all in the same boat. No matter who they'd been before, their shared leprosy now made them outcasts.

Then they heard about a miracle worker named Jesus. In one loud, pitiful voice, they cried out for him to notice and help them. Jesus did, sending them to show the priests their healed bodies—bodies that were being healed of leprosy as they ran.

As they realized what was happening, nine of them ran even faster toward their new lives. But one man stopped. Unlike the others, his first instinct was to run back to Jesus and thank him. So while all the men were blessed with restored bodies, one received a restored soul.

Be sure you never assume a sense of entitlement with God. Think of all he has done for you. Think of all the opportunities he's given you and the many times he's protected you from danger. Most of all, consider that he died on the cross to provide forgiveness for your sins and to give you a brand new life. As you're rushing out to enjoy your blessings, don't forget to stop long enough to say thank you.

WHAT DO YOU THINK WHEN SOMEBODY RECEIVES A FAVOR FROM YOU BUT SHOWS NO GRATITUDE?

READ UP: ISAIAH 12:1–6 • DANIEL 4:34–37

TIRED OF TRYING?

READ AHEAD: MATTHEW 11:25–30

Come to Me, all of you who are weary and burdened, and I will give you rest. Matthew 11:28

Even when you're young and strong, life can wear you down sometimes, both physically and emotionally. There is one form of weariness, however, that no nap, bubble bath, or summer break can touch— *spiritual exhaustion.*

This usually happens gradually and imperceptibly. You might not even be aware that your spiritual strength is draining, but one day you realize your soul feels heavy from all you've experienced. It happens . . .

- When you stop spending time with God as you once did.
- When you allow unconfessed sin or bitterness to weigh you down.
- When you hold on to your anxieties instead of giving them to God.
- When you wrestle with decisions God has already made for you.

These things can subtly eat away at your spiritual strength until you finally hit the wall. You'll know it when it happens, because you'll consider your Christian life a drain—a burden rather than a joy.

It doesn't have to be that way, however. Jesus offers you a perfect, peaceful rest that no human therapy could ever give you. He can give you strength, not only to get back on your feet, but to "soar on wings like eagles" (Isaiah 40:31). He loves you. He wants to carry your burdens. Go to him and find rest for your soul.

HOW CAN YOU TELL WHEN YOU'RE RUNNING LOW ON SPIRITUAL BATTERIES?

READ UP: PSALM 42:1–5 • 2 CORINTHIANS 5:1–15

ANY MORE IDEAS JESUS HAS BEEN TEACHING YOU?

THE POWER OF LOVE

DO THESE TWO WORDS—POWER AND LOVE —BELONG IN THE SAME SENTENCE?

Many of us may not realize it, but we all want power to a certain extent. That's because power means control. Power puts us in the driver's seat. It helps us get what we want. Power is intoxicating.

We go after power in different ways. Some of us try to exert influence on others by using our strength to bully them. Some of us are master manipulators. We use subtle, emotional maneuvers on people to get what we want from them. We may enlist the help of our money or our friends or our status to assist us. But in whatever way we go about getting the upper hand, we do it because we think there is strength in power. Our goal is to dominate others.

Love, on the other hand, strikes us as a much gentler quality. That's why people sometimes mistakenly equate love with weakness. We think doing the loving thing—such as forgiving another person or putting the needs of someone else first—is a sign of giving in, of surrendering control. We're sometimes afraid to love others because it makes us vulnerable. We assume we can either be loving or we can be in control, but we can't be both.

So . . . can love and power coexist?

They do in God! The most powerful One in the universe is also the most loving. In fact, God is *more* than loving. "God is love" (1 John 4:8). His love is so strong that nothing has "the power to separate us" from it (Romans 8:38–39).

Over the next six days, let's see what God has to say about the power of love. And let's see how these two great strengths come together to make us fully alive in Christ.

ROCK SOLID

READ AHEAD: ROMANS 8:31–39

In all these things we are more than victorious through Him who loved us. Romans 8:37

Just about everything in life is subject to change without notice. Your friend can become your enemy. Your home situation can turn intense. Your knee can give out in a basketball game.

Only one thing is guaranteed to remain the same. There is one constant—one thing you can count on, now and forever: the unfailing love of God.

No matter what your situation is right now—whether you're healthy or suffering from disease, on top of the world or feeling like a failure, victorious in Christ or dealing with the consequences of sin—God loves you, no matter what. His love isn't altered by your circumstances. It is steady and unchanging.

If there is anything the Bible makes crystal clear, it is that God loves his children. The apostle Paul tried to imagine a way that God's love could fail, but he couldn't think of one. The psalmist could proclaim, "Give thanks to the Lord, for He is good; His faithful love endures forever" (Psalm 106:1).

You may feel at times that God couldn't possibly love you. You may wonder why a loving God would allow you to go through difficult times. But always remember that God's love is not determined by your state of mind or your current situation. Base your security on this one unchanging truth: nothing can separate you from God's love.

IF GOD'S LOVE CANNOT CHANGE, HOW DOES THAT CHANGE YOUR OUTLOOK ON YOUR FUTURE?

READ UP: NEHEMIAH 9:9–21 • EPHESIANS 3:14–19

TRUE LOVE

READ AHEAD: 1 CORINTHIANS 13:4–8

Love is patient; love is kind. Love does not envy; is not boastful; is not conceited. 1 Corinthians 13:4

The problem with love is that so many people don't have a clue what it is. Love is not a feeling. It's an attitude.

Obviously, basing any human relationship strictly on feelings is asking for trouble. Moms and dads who love their children only when the mood hits them are poor parents. A friend who remains loyal only until a better offer comes along is not much of a friend. A husband who deserts his wife and children because he finds another woman more attractive has missed the point of marriage.

Love is often presented to you as something to be "fallen into" and "fallen out of." But what do you do when the emotion fails you and the warm fuzzies are gone, other than bailing out and starting over with someone else? That's the unpredictable nature of worldly love.

The Bible, however, offers a different kind of love, one that's committed to acting lovingly toward others regardless of how you feel. Biblical love is patient, unselfish, and loyal. It doesn't keep score. It assumes the best motives. It gives without expecting or demanding return. It always seeks to honor God. It endures through thick, thin, and in-between. Biblical love is eternal.

Feelings come and go. Feelings don't last. But ask God to take you beyond the world's way of loving so you can love others in a totally new dimension, as God does.

HAVE YOU SEEN TRUE, GODLY LOVE IN SOMEONE? WHAT DOES IT LOOK LIKE IN REAL LIFE?

READ UP: ROMANS 5:6–8 • 1 JOHN 4:7–12

LOVE ALWAYS

READ AHEAD: 1 CORINTHIANS 16:13–14

Your every action must be done with love. 1 Corinthians 16:14

Christians play by a different set of rules than the world does. The world, for example, says it's good to be honest, moral, and loving, but there are certain times when it's okay to make an exception—like when you're threatened or mistreated. Then the world gives you permission to respond in anger.

The standard for Christians, however, is straightforward. Do everything in love. No qualifiers. No exceptions.

"How is that possible?" you ask. "After all, aren't there times when people hurt you and take advantage of you? Don't you have to look out for yourself?"

If anyone ever had an excuse to make exceptions like these, it was Jesus. People hated him so much, they ridiculed him, betrayed him, tortured him, and killed him. Yet Jesus loved them and forgave them. He always responded in love. Though no one else in human history was as powerful as Jesus was, he never took advantage of another person. He never based his actions on what others did to him or around him. He lived by one truth: love.

As Christ's followers, we too must base our lives on Jesus' standard. A Christian should never be known as an angry or selfish person. The one thing that should characterize each of us is love.

HOW DO THE REWARDS OF LOVING OTHERS COMPARE WITH THE RELIEF OF FIGHTING BACK?

READ UP: JOHN 13:34–35 • ROMANS 12:17–21

LOVE GROWS UP

READ AHEAD: PHILIPPIANS 1:3–11

I pray this: that your love will keep on growing in knowledge and every kind of discernment. Philippians 1:9

Love without discernment—love that doesn't have any thought behind it—is not really love.

Parents, for instance, who show love to their children by overindulging and refusing to discipline are really hurting them in the long run. The guy who asks his girlfriend to prove her love by having sex with him is using her, not loving her. A person who isn't truthful with someone for fear of losing a friendship is not acting as a true friend.

Love has to be discerning. It has to include an awareness of what God wants. It has to seek the best for others.

Is it possible to love like that? Only by letting God help you. He will tell you when to be gentle with someone and when to be firm. The Holy Spirit will help you know when to get involved in someone's problems and when to leave them alone. He will show you how to give without asking for something in return. When you love others this way, you're loving them the way Christ loves them.

So seek to be blameless in all your relationships. This means guarding your thoughts, your words, and your actions to make sure you have the other person's best interests at heart. Ask God to teach you how to love people with discernment, to treat them with a love that comes only from him.

HOW CAN YOU TELL THE DIFFERENCE BETWEEN SENTIMENTAL LOVE AND GENUINE LOVE?

READ UP: 1 SAMUEL 20:1–17 • 1 JOHN 3:16–24

LOVE TAKES TIME

READ AHEAD: LUKE 10:38–42

Lord, don't you care that my sister has left me to serve alone? So tell her to give me a hand. Luke 10:40

We often conclude from this story that Martha was the grump, while Mary was the one with the pure, simple motives. But is sitting around always a better choice than working? What would happen if Christians spent all their time reading the Bible and going to church, but never cleaned their rooms or mowed the grass?

So maybe we're being too hard on Martha . . . and not completely understanding what Jesus was saying.

Martha was showing her love for Jesus by being a good hostess to him. No doubt, she wanted to spend time with her Lord as much as Mary did, but *someone* had to do the work. Perhaps she thought if her sister would help out, they'd *both* have time to sit at Jesus' feet and learn from his teaching. Maybe that's what aggravated Martha the most—hearing the muffled sounds of Jesus' voice in the other room, longing to hear what he was saying, but mad that she was stuck in the kitchen by herself. So the more she worked, the more agitated she grew. Finally, she couldn't stand it any more, and she took her frustrations out on Mary.

Jesus knew that both Mary *and* Martha loved him. But what Martha didn't know was that she didn't have to prove it to him by constantly working. Sure, there are times to be busy, but there are also times to stop doing and start listening.

HOW CAN YOUR EFFORTS AT SERVING JESUS KEEP YOU FROM SPENDING TIME WITH HIM?

READ UP: PSALM 27:4–6 • 1 CORINTHIANS 13:1–3

A LOVE LIKE HIS

READ AHEAD: JOHN 15:9–17

This is My command: love one another as I have loved you.
John 15:12

If we aren't careful, we can begin to adopt the world's way of loving instead of God's. The world says love is a feeling. They say when you stop having feelings for someone, it means you no longer love him, you no longer love her.

But Jesus commanded those who wanted to be his disciples to follow his standard for loving people rather than the world's standard. His standard is to love others in exactly the same way he loves us.

When Jesus saw us hopelessly enslaved to sin, for example, he didn't say, "I don't feel like dying on a cross for them. I think I'll wait until the feeling comes." He didn't say, "I have tried and tried to love them, but they always reject me. I give up!"

Jesus saw that without him we would perish, and he acted lovingly toward us despite our rejecting him. His love did not depend on what we did to deserve it, or even on whether or not we accepted it! Jesus freely and unconditionally gave us his love.

This is how God wants us to love others. Not with strings attached. Not just to love as long as they are lovable. Not just to love as long as they appreciate it. God wants us to give our love freely, unconditionally. Only he can help us love people in this way.

Today, ask Christ to love others through you . . . even those who aren't easy to love.

WHAT WOULD YOU DO DIFFERENTLY IF YOU LOVED PEOPLE THE WAY JESUS DOES?

READ UP: MATTHEW 5:43–48 • LUKE 19:1–10

WHAT'S YOUR DEFINITION OF LOVE NOW?

INSIDE THE PSALMS

Reading the Psalms is like holding a mirror up to life. There is so much to see—all the things you'd expect from the Scripture, but also every emotion and experience known to man: worship, anger, sorrow, depression, joy, grief, honor, defeat, prayer, brokenness.

Life is not a flat line. Even the Christian life has its ups and downs. Everyone goes through times of victory and times of failure, times of celebration and times of mourning.

That's why as you study the Psalms, you'll be able to relate to the words you're reading, because they come straight from the hearts of those who wrote them. David wrote many of the Psalms—some in caves as he hid from a demented and dangerous enemy, others during times of great joy and triumph, praising God for his power, justice, faithfulness, and deliverance.

So regardless of whether you're experiencing good times or bad times today, the Psalms have a message for you. They'll give you an example of what it means to love God in all situations and to trust him in spite of your circumstances. As you walk through a few of these Psalms over the course of the next eleven devotions, you'll learn more about your own relationship with God . . . how to be free to experience him, to enjoy him, and to entrust each moment of your life to him. In one place, we're even going to ask you to read the famous 23rd Psalm several days in a row, so it will never be merely words to you ever again.

Some people have the wrong perception that walking with God is dull, boring, and repressive. But the Psalms, so full of force and passion, break the mold on tired, tasteless Christianity.

THE WAY TO BLESSING

READ AHEAD: PSALM 1:1–6

How happy is the man who does not follow the advice of the wicked, or take the path of sinners, or join a group of mockers.
Psalm 1:1

It's no accident why some people consistently receive God's blessing on their lives while others do not. Is it because God loves some of us more than others? Of course not. What is the difference then? It all depends on people's choices.

The Bible says there are things we can do (or avoid doing) that will determine God's blessings in our lives. Take the friends we choose, for example. If we allow sinful people to influence us, we shouldn't be surprised when God doesn't bless our lives. It's impossible to spend prolonged time in the company of ungodly people without being affected by their sinful attitudes. Even if our motivation is to provide a positive influence on them, we need to have our eyes wide open or the influence will end up going the wrong way.

On the other hand, if we choose the friends we know God wants us to have, we'll find our lives overflowing with blessings. As we spend time with those whose lives please God, we'll find the strength and encouragement to live pure, meaningful lives ourselves. As we seek direction from God's Word, we'll not wander down dangerous roads that lead only to despair. We'll know where we're headed, and we won't be lured off the right path by others.

God does not arbitrarily choose to bless one person and not another. We determine by our own choices whether or not we will open up our lives to the good things God has in store for us.

HOW HAVE YOU SEEN FRIENDS CHANGING PEOPLE FOR THE BETTER? FOR THE WORSE?

READ UP: 1 KINGS 12:1–14 • MARK 2:1–5

BIG PRAYERS

READ AHEAD: PSALM 2:7–12

Ask of Me, and I will make the nations Your inheritance and the ends of the earth Your possession. Psalm 2:8

Do you pray big or do you pray small? If you pray big, you understand what God is like: powerful, almighty, all-knowing, eternal. If you pray small, could it be you're afraid God can't deliver? Because the more you understand who God is, the bigger your prayer life will grow.

Think about the way you pray. If you never ask God for anything more than a good day, or for your friend's cold to get better, you're missing out on much of what God wants to do in your life. He wants to give you more than a good day. He wants to give you the ends of the earth!

Don't doubt that God wants to do big things in your life. Pray with confidence. Pray with anticipation. If you pray little prayers, you'll get little answers.

If God hasn't been doing anything big in your life, it's not because he's not able. God is not a distant, untouchable being. He's more willing to be involved in your life than you might think. It may be that you simply haven't asked him.

So when you pray, go beyond vague, safe prayers, such as "Lord, be with me today." That kind of prayer is a given. Think about the one you're addressing as you pray. God is big! So don't be afraid to pray big!

WHAT WOULD BE AN EXAMPLE OF A BIG PRAYER TO YOU?

READ UP: MATTHEW 7:7–11 • EPHESIANS 3:20–21

ALL DAY LONG

READ AHEAD: PSALM 5:1–3

At daybreak, Lord, You hear my voice; at daybreak I plead my case to You and watch expectantly. Psalm 5:3

What you do next after you've prayed reveals what you really believe about God.

If you pray in the morning for your unbelieving friend to become a Christian, but then don't share your faith with him when God gives you the opportunity, you've merely recited a prayer. You haven't really prayed.

If you ask God in the morning to increase your faith, but then don't look for the opportunities he'll give you to trust him, you don't understand what prayer really is.

When David prayed to God every morning, he didn't get up off of his knees and go about his day as if he'd never prayed. No, he watched in anticipation for the answer he knew would come. He prepared himself to obey whatever God asked him to do next. That's the difference between just saying prayers and truly praying. Prayer is not an isolated event. It's an ongoing activity that flows out of your relationship with God.

If you've been in the habit of reciting prayers instead of truly praying, you've been practicing a ritual, not enjoying a relationship. When God speaks to you in the morning, or when the Holy Spirit prompts you to pray for something, watch expectantly throughout the day for God's answer. Walking with God is not something you do for fifteen minutes each morning before getting on with your life. Walking with God *is* your life! It's an exciting adventure to be lived all day long!

WHAT DO YOU THINK IT MEANS TO "PRAY CONSTANTLY"? (1 THESSALONIANS 5:17)

READ UP: 1 KINGS 3:4–15 • 1 JOHN 5:14–15

A GOOD NIGHT'S SLEEP

READ AHEAD: PSALM 3:1–6

I lie down and sleep; I wake again because the Lord sustains me.
Psalm 3:5

David could easily have turned into an insomniac, because he had so many people after him day and night, trying to take his life. On the contrary, however, he slept like a baby because he knew his life was in God's hands. He was able to let his guard down because he was confident God was watching over him.

It's our nature to think we're solely responsible for our own well-being, but trying to stand guard over our own lives is futile for two reasons:

1) We're not always aware of the dangers around us.

2) Even if we know what we're up against, we don't always have the power to do anything about it.

That's where anxiety comes in. We fear what we don't know and what we can't control. We find it hard to sleep at night because we're preoccupied with our present situation or afraid of what tomorrow might bring. We spend needless hours tossing and turning. But when we learn to hand our anxieties over to God and let *him* stand guard over our lives, we find the peace and security that lets us rest.

If you find yourself fretting about what's happening around you, or if you seem to be consistently worrying about tomorrow, take the night off. Get some sleep and let God relieve you of your post. He's far more qualified for the job than you are.

WHAT'S THE DIFFERENCE BETWEEN CONCERN AND WORRY?

READ UP: PSALM 91:1–13 • ISAIAH 41:8–10

PRIORITY LIST

READ AHEAD: PSALM 5:4–12

You, Lord, bless the righteous one; You surround him with favor like a shield. Psalm 5:12

To have a close walk with God, you have to live by the right priorities. Let's take a look at David's priorities—a man who knew God better than most people did:

• *Worship.* David didn't merely go to the temple as a matter of ritual. He considered it a great privilege to be invited into the presence of holy God, to "bow down" to him in "reverential awe" (verse 7).

• *Confession.* David wasn't perfect by a long shot. In fact, he committed some pretty major sins, including adultery and murder. However, he couldn't bear to be separated from God by his own sinfulness. He prayed, "Lord, lead me in Your righteousness" (verse 8).

• *Submission.* David was a gifted leader and an accomplished warrior, yet he consistently turned to God for guidance. He understood that life was too complicated for even the smartest person to figure out on his own. He needed God to make the way "straight" before him (verse 8).

• *Dependence.* David had plenty of enemies and plenty to fear. He prayed daily for God's protection, and he relied on God for peace in spite of his tumultuous life. He considered the Lord his "refuge" and "shelter" (verse 11).

• *Gratitude.* David's life was characterized by thankfulness. He recognized God as the source of every blessing in his life, and he developed a habit of thanking God regularly. The book of Psalms is a record of David's grateful heart.

WHAT ARE SOME OF THE ITEMS ON YOUR PRIORITY LIST?

READ UP: DEUTERONOMY 30:15–20 • HEBREWS 13:15–18

SATISFIED SHEEP

READ AHEAD: PSALM 23:1–6

The Lord is my shepherd; there is nothing I lack. Psalm 23:1

According to the Scriptures, it's a whole lot better to be a sheep than to be a lion.

• Lions are fierce and strong. Sheep are weak and defenseless, but they don't have to fear for their safety.

• Lions are mighty hunters, yet sheep don't go hungry. That's because the sheep have something the lions don't have—a shepherd.

• Lions must depend upon their own strength and cunning, but sheep belong to someone who will lay down his very life for their safety.

Psalm 34:10 observes: "Young lions lack food and go hungry, but those who seek the Lord will not lack any good thing." In other words, even the strongest, most ambitious people may not always have all they need, but those who trust God to provide for them will have all their needs met . . . and more!

God himself is the greatest security you have. No enemy can succeed against you when you are under God's care. You will never lose your way in life when God is the one guiding you. No crisis you face will be too difficult for God to overcome. It's all a matter of where you put your trust.

If you wander away from your Shepherd, you will miss out on what the Shepherd wants to give you. But under his care, you will find strength, purpose, and security. He is the only one you can always depend on to meet your needs.

WHAT HAPPENS WHEN YOU PUT YOUR TRUST IN CHURCH, OR RELIGION, OR EVEN IN OTHER CHRISTIANS?

READ UP: PSALM 139:7–12 • JOHN 10:11–18

GREEN PASTURES

READ AHEAD: PSALM 23:1-6

He lets me lie down in green pastures; He leads me beside quiet waters. Psalm 23:2

Some people will gladly run your life for you if you let them! Some people have a way of always bringing you down rather than building you up. They encourage you to get involved in destructive things. They take advantage of you. They're mainly interested in what you can give *them*, not what they can give you.

But there is another kind of friend—someone who actually cares about what's best for you.

It may be a parent, teacher, classmate, coach, teammate, pastor—anyone God brings alongside you to help you make smart choices. These friends are your "green pastures," your "quiet waters." They are God's provision for you. They will encourage you to slow down when you take on too much. They will challenge you to get busy when you're too idle. They care about you enough to warn you when you're heading into danger.

God knows exactly what you need and when you need it. That's why he has placed people around you who can guide you along the best path. So if you're finding that your Christian life is wearing you out and leaving you distressed, look to see if you've wandered away from the "green pastures" and "quiet waters" your Shepherd has provided you. God will see that you're equipped with all the spiritual help you need.

If you know you've been wandering in the wrong direction, return to the Shepherd. He wants to give you peace and rest.

HOW CAN YOU BE GOD'S GIFT OF REFRESHMENT TO SOMEONE YOU KNOW?

READ UP: DEUTERONOMY 3:27-28 • ROMANS 1:8-12

RESTORING YOUR SOUL

READ AHEAD: PSALM 23:1–6

He renews my life; He leads me along the right paths for His name's sake. Psalm 23:3

Do you sometimes feel spiritually worn out? It can happen to anyone.

Maybe you're carrying an unusually heavy load of problems. Perhaps you've been battling a nagging temptation, or you've been on the receiving end of unfair criticism. Whatever it is, it has beaten you down. Deep within your soul, there's a weariness that you think you can't overcome.

Spiritual exhaustion can catch you by surprise. It happens gradually. And before you know it, you've become disoriented to God. Perhaps you've gotten so far from God that you're not sure you even care about spiritual things anymore. Your problems have distracted you from spending time with God as you used to, and now he seems like a stranger.

But God has a way of strengthening you at the deepest levels of your life. His Spirit searches out the most private corners of your mind to renew your thinking. Your Good Shepherd can lead you to people and to places where you'll be refreshed and energized. God may teach you something about himself that will give you a new excitement about being a Christian. He'll give you a fresh start.

The way he chooses to restore you will be as unique as you are, but your Shepherd will always revitalize your soul if you ask him. Don't be afraid to ask.

WHAT ARE SOME OF THE FIRST WARNING SIGNS THAT YOU'RE SLIPPING AWAY FROM GOD?

READ UP: HOSEA 6:1–3 • ZECHARIAH 10:1–7

SHADOWS

READ AHEAD: PSALM 23:1–6

Even when I go through the darkest valley, I fear no danger, for You are with me; Your rod and Your staff—they comfort me.
Psalm 23:4

David's beautiful psalm about the Good Shepherd is one of the Bible's most well-known passages. In fact, it's probably read or recited as much *outside* of church as in it. Truly, this inspiring message of hope speaks in a way that all of us can understand.

David did what every good writer does: he wrote about what he knew. He knew lots about life's shadows, plus he was intimately acquainted with shepherding. So he masterfully joined the two together to pen some of the most comforting words of hope ever written.

David faced many dangers in his life—times when he didn't know if he'd live out the day; times when he was misunderstood, threatened, and attacked; times when the shame of his own sin sent him into the depths of despair. Yet through it all, he experienced the unwavering presence of God.

Just as he once led his sheep through the valleys, David's Shepherd guided him through the dark times in his life. Just as David's sheep used to recognize his voice through the darkness and follow the sound, God's voice brought comfort and direction to David when he didn't know where to go.

Life is full of shadows. There's evil out there—dangers and frightening valleys where the mountains block out the light. But Jesus, your Good Shepherd, will walk with you through the valleys and dispel the shadows of fear.

WHAT GOOD THINGS HAVE YOU BEEN KEPT FROM ENJOYING BECAUSE OF FEAR?

READ UP: ISAIAH 43:1–2 • 1 CORINTHIANS 15:51–58

BATTLE RESTED

READ AHEAD: PSALM 23:1–6

You prepare a table before me in the presence of my enemies; You anoint my head with oil; my cup overflows. Psalm 23:5

Soldiers don't usually sit down for a picnic in the middle of a raging battlefield. They either fight to the death, or they turn and run!

But David painted a very different kind of battlefield scene—a picture of total security. In the midst of the worst onslaughts his enemies could dish out, David found peace in God and a reason to celebrate. Others were trying to keep the crown from him, but they couldn't stop God from making him king.

Going through life's hardest battles can sometimes teach us the most about God. When our enemies are attacking us and we want to panic, God gives us peace. He lays out a banquet to celebrate the victory that's already ours. He reminds us who we are in Christ: a royal treasure claimed by the King as his own.

When everything is going well, we might take God's presence for granted, but when life is hard, we can often see his presence more clearly. That's because he gives us peace and cause for celebration in places where we'd expect only despair.

If you're experiencing some of the difficulties that life throws at you, look to see what God is doing. He hasn't gone anywhere. He's preparing a table for your victory party, pouring out his blessings on you. You don't have to leave the battlefield to have your picnic, because God is with you . . . and your enemies don't intimidate him.

WHAT'S WRONG WITH THE IDEA THAT A LOVING GOD WOULD NEVER ALLOW HARDSHIP INTO OUR LIVES?

READ UP: HABAKKUK 3:17–19 • 1 PETER 4:12–19

GOD IS GOOD

READ AHEAD: PSALM PSALM 23:1–6

Only goodness and faithful love will pursue me all the days of my life, and I will dwell in the house of the Lord as long as I live.
Psalm 23:6

We run into trouble when we try to look through our circumstances to understand what God is like. If we have a bad day, for example, we might conclude that God doesn't love us. If it's a *really* bad day, we may even decide God is picking on us. When things are going well, though, we might assume God has just decided to be good to us for a day.

But if circumstances determined God's character, David would have wanted to run as far away from the house of the Lord as he could, not dwell in it! He lived through some terrible hardships! Yet he discovered that the right perspective gave him a completely different view of his life. He was free to experience God deeply in both good times and in bad.

People say we can only count on two things in life: death and taxes. Maybe so, but we Christians can add two more absolutes to our lives, and it's important for us to establish these truths firmly in our hearts once and for all:

- God loves us
- And God is good to us.

Don't focus on your problems and miss God's goodness. Take note of the many ways he's expressing his love to you in spite of your problems or even through them. When you look at life from the right perspective, you'll see God as he really is.

WHAT DOES IT MEAN TO "DWELL IN THE HOUSE OF THE LORD" FOR AS LONG AS YOU LIVE?

READ UP: PSALM 84:1–4 • 2 PETER 1:3–11

WRITE OUT PSALM 23 IN YOUR OWN WORDS.

_____

_____

_____

_____

_____

_____

_____

_____

_____

_____

_____

_____

_____

_____

_____

_____

_____

_____

_____

_____

_____

LEARNING FROM PAUL

Do you know people who make you want to follow Christ more closely —just by being around them?

Some people have lived such diverse and interesting lives, filled with so many rich experiences and courageous stories, you could just talk with them all day long and never get tired of it.

It's the same way when you spend time with people who are truly wise—people who walk closely with God. You find yourself motivated to live *your* life more fully as well. God's power is so evident in some people that you feel yourself drawn to them. You learn from them, and you're a better person because you know them.

Paul was that kind of person. He'd seen it all. He'd been everywhere. He'd witnessed miracles and experienced miracles himself. He spoke God's word with authority and boldness. He was so good at making an articulate case for Christianity, exposing the holes in godless or religious logic by using his powerful gifts of faith and intellect.

And even though he ruffled the feathers of many, even though he could be controversial and confrontational at times, he endeared people to himself . . . by endearing people to his Lord, by presenting Christ with so much strength and life and energy.

As you spend the next twelve days of devotions with Paul, understand that you're learning from a well-traveled and very wise man. He has a lot of good advice for you. So enjoy your time with Paul. You won't easily forget what he has to say!

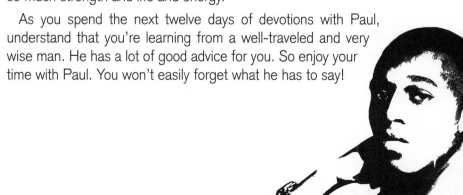

YOUR FATHER

READ AHEAD: ROMANS 8:12–17

The Spirit Himself testifies together with our spirit that we are God's children. Romans 8:16

Your personality is partly the result of the way you were parented. Other factors are also involved, of course, but parents have a bigger influence on their children than some like to admit.

Children from abusive homes, for example, usually suffer from severe insecurity. They may struggle with anger in much the same way their parents do, repeating the cycle when they have children of their own. On the other hand, parents who are kind and loving tend to pass on these traits to their children.

When you become a Christian, you are adopted by a perfect Parent —a heavenly Father who loves you unconditionally. You have nothing to fear from him, because he watches over you with constant love and protection. He is more powerful than any problem you will ever face. You will not live in want, because your Father's resources are unlimited.

As God's child, then, your life ought to reflect his character. The more time you spend with your Father, the more you'll become like him: loving, patient, giving, and fair. As you grow in your faith, His influence will come to have even more of an impact on you than your earthly parents do.

So don't use imperfect parents as an excuse for not living up to God's standards. You *do* have a perfect Parent who will teach you how to be loving, forgiving, patient, and everything else—just like he is.

HOW MUCH TIME HAVE YOU BEEN SPENDING WITH YOUR FATHER LATELY?

READ UP: JOHN 17:24–26 • GALATIANS 4:3–7

I CAN WAIT

READ AHEAD: ROMANS 8:18–25

*I consider that the sufferings of this present time are not worth
comparing with the glory that is going to be revealed to us.*
Romans 8:18

Many of Paul's friends suffered because they were Christians. Some
lost their jobs. Others were beaten. Many were killed.

In light of the dangers involved, some of them questioned whether
Christianity was worth it. It would be easier, they figured, to at least be
silent Christians, outwardly following the crowd to avoid persecution.
Paul assured them, however, that everything they were going through
was worth it. He promised that their present suffering would be more
than compensated for by the rewards that awaited them in heaven.

In light of an eternity in heaven, this life is only a blip on the screen. If
only we could fully understand how magnificent heaven will be! No tears.
No pain. No suffering. When we reach our eternal home, we will realize
that everything the Bible said was true. Everything God promised will be
ours. Then we will know that living the Christian life was well worth the
effort.

If you're going through a difficult time right now, keep in mind that this
life is only temporary. Nothing you might be suffering now can compare
to the reward you will receive for having patiently endured.

So don't become disheartened by the problems you face right now.
God has things for you to learn and to do for him. Remain faithful to him
today, and your reward in heaven will be beyond comparison!

SPEND A FEW MINUTES TRYING TO IMAGINE ETERNITY. WHAT DO YOU THINK OF?

READ UP: 1 THESSALONIANS 4:13–18 • REVELATION 21:1–7

IT'S ALL GOOD

READ AHEAD: ROMANS 8:28–29

We know that all things work together for the good of those who love God: those who are called according to His purpose.
Romans 8:28

People often misunderstand Romans 8:28. Some assume that this promise means God will turn every bad situation into a good situation. But the Bible doesn't say that. It says that God can *use* any situation—even the worst experience—to produce good results in a Christian's life.

Some also misunderstand this verse by assuming it applies to everyone. It doesn't. It is only for those who "love" God and have been "called" by him. If you are angry at God or do not love him, he doesn't promise to work all your experiences out for good.

Paul knew what he was talking about. He had endured some horrid experiences: insults, threats, beatings, arrests, stonings, shipwrecks. Yet in every bad situation, God brought about something good. For example, as a result of Paul's imprisonment, a jailer found new life in Christ (Acts 16:22–40). As a result of being arrested and hauled off to Rome, Paul was able to proclaim Christ in "Caesar's household" (Philippians 4:22).

If you're seeking to do what God has called you to do, the promise of Romans 8:28 is for you. Whatever experiences you go through, whether good or bad, you can have confidence that God will bring something good out of them.

Don't expect God to remove every difficult situation. Watch instead to see how he uses the tough times to bring about good in your life.

CAN YOU THINK OF A TIME WHEN YOU LEANED ON THE PROMISE OF THIS VERSE?

READ UP: GENESIS 50:15–21 • JEREMIAH 29:10–14

BACK TALK

READ AHEAD: ROMANS 9:14–24

Who are you—anyone who talks back to God? Will what is formed say to the one who formed it, "Why did you make me like this?"
Romans 9:20

Asking questions is a natural part of growing up. When you were younger, you probably accepted things more readily than you do now. But as you grow toward independence, you begin to think more for yourself. You no longer want others to make your decisions for you.

Paul warned, however, that there is one line you should never cross: you should never challenge God's wisdom. No one has the right to talk back to the Lord of the universe.

God is in control of all that exists, including you. He has had a plan for your life since before you were born. This plan is as unique as you are, and it involves the very best that God has to give you. Don't get caught up in comparing your place in God's plan to the one he has for others. That will make you either proud or envious. You'll lose sight of the truth that God loves *you* just as much as he loves your friends.

Just as the potter has total mastery over the clay in his hands, God has the absolute right to your life. He wants to mold you and stretch you to suit his plan for you. That is his right as your Creator.

So trust him. He knows what he's doing. Choose to serve the Lord cheerfully in everything you do, no matter how mundane, and you will discover the secret to a joyful, meaningful life.

WHAT HAVE YOU BEEN TEMPTED TO COMPLAIN TO GOD ABOUT LATELY?

READ UP: JOB 42:1–6 • 2 CORINTHIANS 4:7–11

JESUS IS LORD

READ AHEAD: ROMANS 10:5–10

*If you confess with your mouth, "Jesus is Lord," and believe in
your heart that God raised Him from the dead, you will be saved.*
Romans 10:9

Many people think receiving Christ is a complicated process, but salvation requires only two things: belief and confession. Believe in your heart that Jesus is who he said he was, and willingly share this truth with others. Then you will know you are a Christian.

Millions of people through the centuries have proclaimed Jesus as Lord without following him personally. They have declared Christ to be God without ever believing he could make a difference in their lives. Their words were empty because what they said wasn't backed up by personal faith. Sadly, words without faith are not enough.

Likewise, the Bible doesn't recognize Christians who are secret about it. Believing that Jesus is alive and risen from the dead is only part of the equation. According to Paul, true followers of Jesus will confess him before others.

Confessing Christ doesn't require eloquent speeches or theological training. It simply requires acknowledging before others that we know Jesus, not only as Lord of all but as Lord and master over us personally. In Paul's day, confessing Christ was dangerous business. Today, however, we are free to declare our allegiance to Jesus in ways that Paul never could have imagined.

Christianity is a living faith, a combination of believing and confessing. You can't get much clearer than Romans 10:9.

HOW CAN YOU MAKE YOUR FAITH MORE OF A PUBLIC CONFESSION?

READ UP: MATTHEW 10:32–39 • 2 TIMOTHY 1:8–12

43

SOMETHING FOR EVERYONE

READ AHEAD: ROMANS 10:11–17

Faith comes from what is heard, and what is heard comes through the message about Christ. Romans 10:17

We tend to make two mistakes that limit our effectiveness in telling people about Jesus.

• Mistake #1: *We assume that everyone has heard the gospel.*

After all, Christianity is everywhere. How could they not have heard? But if we actually knew how many people around us have no idea who Jesus really is, it would astound us. Christianity was brand new in Paul's day, so he saw everyone as someone who needed to hear about Christ for the first time. Our generation too often assumes that because we have heard the gospel, others have heard it too. This error in our thinking causes us to miss many opportunities to share our faith.

• Mistake #2: *We assume some people are so hard, they'd never accept Christ's love.*

Paul knew better. Paul had topped the list of least-likely candidates for salvation, yet Christ had softened Paul's heart and completely turned his life around. The Bible says that salvation is available to everyone, no matter how young or old or how deeply caught up in sin.

It's critical that we understand, as Paul did, that others are depending on us to tell them the good news. The only thing that prevents some people from knowing Christ's love is our unwillingness to share it. Look around you today. Is there someone who needs to hear the good news of Christ?

WHAT'S THE WORST THING THAT COULD HAPPEN TO YOU IF YOU SHARED CHRIST WITH SOMEONE TODAY?

READ UP: 1 CORINTHIANS 2:1–5 • 1 PETER 3:13–17

AGAINST THE FLOW

READ AHEAD: ROMANS 12:1–8

Do not be conformed to this age, but be transformed by the renewing of your mind. Romans 12:2

Don't let the world have a voice in your values. If you let that happen, non-Christians will determine how you think, how you spend your money, and how you spend your time. The world will tell you what's important in life and what your priorities should be.

Don't think so? Turn on your TV. Flip through a magazine. Read the newspaper.

But the media isn't the only way the world wants to squeeze you into its mold. Think about what the non-Christians you know best are most interested in. Then think about your own values. Do they reflect God's priorities, or do they look more like the world's way of thinking? Is there any difference in the way you live and the way an unbeliever lives?

Paul said there's a way to prevent the world's thinking patterns from taking over your own: offer yourself every day to God. Just as Old Testament believers gave animals on the altar as gifts to God, make your life a living sacrifice every day. As you get up each morning, say to God, "Here is my body, my mind, my heart, my time, and my money. Everything belongs to you."

When you turn your life over to God, the Holy Spirit will clean out the garbage in your mind and replace it with God's Word. He will transform you by renewing your mind. The world will no longer determine the way you live. Instead, your life will be an act of worship that brings glory to God each day.

WHAT'S THE APPEAL OF BEING LIKE EVERYONE ELSE?

READ UP: JOSHUA 24:14–15 • EPHESIANS 4:17–24

LOVE/HATE RELATIONSHIP

READ AHEAD: ROMANS 12:9–16

Love must be without hypocrisy. Detest evil; cling to what is good.
Romans 12:9

The Christian life is not nearly so complicated as we sometimes make it out to be. It really comes down to two things:

- Hate what is evil.
- Love what is good.

You know the difference between good and evil. The Bible pictures evil as being darkness, and righteousness as being light. Even the world separates good from evil in its movies and books.

From Adam and Eve—and down through the centuries—evil has been systematically destroying people. It has caused humanity to lie, cheat, steal, abuse, and even kill one another. Only God knows all the suffering that evil has inflicted on people throughout history. And that's why he hates the evil in our lives—because it brings us pain and heartache. He loves us enough to hate what evil does to us.

The more you become like Christ, the more you should see evil for what it is. You should not simply avoid it. You should despise it, as Christ does. You should hate sin for what it does to you and to others. You should have no tolerance for it in your own life. Rather, as Paul said, you should cling to what is good.

Have you become comfortable around evil? Are you tolerating sin in your life? Ask God to give you a holy aversion to sin.

WHAT SINS DO YOU HAVE THE HARDEST TIME HATING?

READ UP: PSALM 51:1–13 • 1 THESSALONIANS 5:15–25

IOUs

READ AHEAD: ROMANS 13:7–10

Do not owe anyone anything, except to love one another.
Romans 13:8

There are all kinds of people in the world. Some are easygoing and are definitely not the worrying type. They have a casual attitude about everything. Their live-and-let-live attitude saves them from anxiety, but it can also make them irresponsible. They don't always consider the way they treat others. They're late for appointments. They break their promises and borrow things without returning them.

Then there are others who lean toward the opposite extreme—ultra-responsible people who keep a mental account of everything they do for others. They put heavy demands on themselves, but they can also be pretty demanding of others. They're always keeping score, and they always know whose turn it is.

The Bible says that Christians shouldn't fall into either category. We should be careful how we treat others. We should respect their time and their possessions. We should be true to our word and honest in our dealings.

This means we won't cheat. It means we repay what we borrow, and we give to others whatever God asks us to give them. It means we pull our weight rather than being a burden to others. The bottom line is this: we are called to be considerate of others.

Do you tend to be undependable? Or are you a demanding scorekeeper? If you lean either way, pray that God will help you to show proper respect to those around you.

HOW IS YOUR RESPECT FOR OTHER PEOPLE A REFLECTION OF YOUR RESPECT FOR GOD?

READ UP: 1 SAMUEL 24:1–7 • 1 TIMOTHY 4:11–16

RIGHT'S AND WRONGS

READ AHEAD: ROMANS 14:13–23

We must pursue what promotes peace and what builds up one another. Romans 14:19

Which is more important to you—to win an argument or to win a friend? Do you know someone who always has to be right, no matter how trivial the debate? How do you feel when you're with someone who's always pointing out your faults?

Some people cause disruption wherever they go. They look at life as a contest, always sizing up the competition. Everyone becomes their rival. The only way they think they can win is by disqualifying everyone else. Disruptive people love to argue, because it gives them a chance to show they're the smartest. They love to criticize because it makes them look better than others by comparison.

Even Christians sometimes act this way. In fact, sin causes all of us to be contentious at times. But dissension does not come from God. It is rooted in our own insecurity—our hungry desire to prove how good or how right we are.

Christians are commanded instead to bring peace wherever we go. God calls us to look for ways to build other people up rather than tearing them down.

Do you struggle with a critical or argumentative spirit? If so, give it over to God. Ask him to help you see others as he sees them. Ask him to make you a peacemaker, one who looks for ways to bring good to others.

WHAT SHOULD KEEP A CHILD OF GOD FROM EVER FEELING INSECURE?

READ UP: PSALM 34:12–14 • 2 TIMOTHY 2:22–26

LET ME HELP YOU

READ AHEAD: ROMANS 15:1-6

We who are strong have an obligation to bear the weaknesses of those without strength, and not to please ourselves. Romans 15:1

The world loves to divide people into two camps: rich and poor, smart and dumb, attractive and ugly, strong and weak. Usually, only one of the two categories is considered desirable. The strong, for example, usually rule the weak.

The Bible, however—as it often does—turns worldly thinking completely around. The Bible tells Christians that the strong are not to dominate the weak but to serve them!

You may be a strong Christian. Perhaps you were raised in a Christian family and you have extensive Bible knowledge. Maybe someone in your church family took extra time to teach you God's ways.

Therefore, you may grow frustrated with weaker Christians who constantly seem to struggle with issues you dealt with long ago. Things that have no power over you may still tempt them. You may grow impatient and be inclined to leave them behind as you move forward in your Christian life. But Paul said that's not the way Christians operate.

The Bible recognizes that some people are stronger than others are. Some have been Christians longer, or have had good role models, or have simply put in more effort. In any case, God expects them to help the weaker Christians around them. Christians show true strength when they help carry their brothers and sisters, not when they forge on ahead, oblivious to the needs of those who are struggling.

WHAT ARE SOME WAYS YOU CAN OFFER YOUR STRENGTH AND ENCOURAGEMENT TO OTHERS?

READ UP: 2 KINGS 6:8-17 • 1 CORINTHIANS 10:23-33

ONE FOCUS

READ AHEAD: ROMANS 16:17–20

I want you to be wise about what is good, yet innocent about what is evil. Romans 16:19

Is there anyone, anywhere, who has it all together? Paul had some good advice for people who think they do: no matter how strong they are, there's always a weak spot somewhere.

The church in Rome was earning a reputation as a sturdy, obedient bunch of believers, but Paul saw potential danger around the corner. He warned the Romans about those who would come and try to deceive them into disobeying God. Paul must have had some concerns about the church's gullibility, for he cautioned them about smooth-talkers who could "deceive the hearts of the unsuspecting" (verse 18).

Paul's advice to the Romans is well taken by us also. No matter how far we've come, we're never all the way there. Just as in Paul's day, deceivers are always around, trying to cause division between us and our fellow believers.

To counteract this, however, many Christians spend far too much time becoming experts in evil. They seek to learn everything they can about Satan in order to avoid his snares. They end up thinking, reading, and talking more about evil than about God.

God doesn't ask for blind obedience from us, but he does want us to be completely innocent of evil. So we should spend our efforts, not being frightened or glamorized by wickedness, but getting to know God through his Word, testing everything we hear against the Scriptures, and avoiding anything that has the appearance of evil.

WHAT'S SO ATTRACTIVE ABOUT BEING UP ON THE BAD THINGS PEOPLE ARE DOING?

READ UP: 2 TIMOTHY 3:1–5 • HEBREWS 3:12–14

50

WHAT ARE THE BIGGEST THINGS YOU'VE LEARNED FROM PAUL?

THE PROVERBS APPEAL

For someone who ended up as a wealthy and powerful king, Solomon had a rather inauspicious beginning.

His mother was Bathsheba, the woman King David lured into an adulterous relationship. You'll remember that in a futile attempt to cover up their affair, David went so far as to have Bathsheba's husband murdered. But in punishing David for these deliberate sins of passion, God allowed the child they had conceived to die.

Their second son, however, was a boy named Solomon. He wasn't the famous soldier his father had been. In fact, he seemed an unlikely choice to replace the greatest warrior king in Israel's history. Some considered Solomon unfit to be the ruler of Israel . . . and even conspired to keep him from attaining the throne.

Imagine, then, that you were Solomon, facing these same challenges. If God came to you with an open invitation, telling you to ask for whatever you wished, what would your prayer have been?

Make me a valiant warrior like my father?

Destroy my enemies? Bring peace to Israel?

Grant me health and a long life?

Give me wealth and every pleasure known to man?

Solomon asked for none of these things. He decided that with all the temptations and decisions he faced, the best thing he could ask for was wisdom—a request which pleased God so much, he gave him wisdom along with everything else he could have requested.

The book of Proverbs, largely written by Solomon, contains some of the finest, most practical insights found anywhere in literature. We're going to take a long stretch of time looking at them, learning from a man who received his wisdom directly from God.

WHERE WISDOM COMES FROM

READ AHEAD: PROVERBS 1:1–6

A wise man will listen and increase his learning, and a discerning man will obtain guidance. Proverbs 1:5

Most of us want all we can get out of life. After all, we only have one life to live! Unless we are wise in our decision making, though, we can waste the one life we have.

Solomon said that a wise person is continually learning more. The more he learns, the more a wise person realizes how much is still left to discover. The more knowledge she gains, the more a wise person understands her potential and the more she is able to give to share with others.

On the other hand, some people try to get by with the least amount of learning possible. They exert only enough effort in school to get by. They never read or study anything they don't have to. They rarely ask questions. They're indifferent to what's happening around them. Solomon called these people fools.

But a wise person "walks with the wise" (Proverbs 13:20). He seeks out the company of mature people. She reads, asks questions, and seizes opportunities to learn more about the wonders of life.

So while you're young, make it a habit to spend time with the wisest people you know. Observe their lives and ask them lots of questions, being careful to spend more time listening than talking. The knowledge you gain will enable you to live your life to the maximum. Don't live life as a fool. Life is far too important to live carelessly.

WHAT WOULD YOU HAVE TO GIVE UP TO BEGIN INVESTING YOUR TIME IN LEARNING AND LISTENING?

READ UP: 2 KINGS 2:1–15 • 2 TIMOTHY 3:10–15

WHAT ARE YOU AFRAID OF?

READ AHEAD: PROVERBS 1:7–9

The fear of the Lord is the beginning of knowledge;
fools despise wisdom and instruction. Proverbs 1:7

We often read this phrase in the Bible: "Do not be afraid." Yet Solomon said that fear can be a good thing. Fear is where knowledge begins. God gives his wisdom to those who "fear" him—those who realize who they are compared to who he is.

Spend a few minutes thinking about what God is like:

• *He is powerful.* He created an entire universe from nothing!

• *He is all-knowing,* aware of your every action and mood, your hopes and dreams, your every thought.

• *He is timeless.* He has always existed, and he always will. Being the creator of time, he is not bound by it as we are.

It really is too amazing to grasp, isn't it? But equally as incredible is the knowledge that God loves us more than we could ever understand. It seems inconceivable that he longs for a close, personal relationship with each of us—the very creatures who sent Jesus to the cross. This knowledge ought to make us tremble, not in the fear that God would hurt us, but in awe of his magnificence.

When we begin to understand who God is—what he has done for us and what he is really like—we have started down the path to wisdom. Solomon said it best: only a fool would refuse such an opportunity.

WHY MUST FEAR BE PART OF A HEALTHY RELATIONSHIP WITH GOD?

READ UP: ECCLESIASTES 12:13–14 • REVELATION 15:1–4

YANKED AROUND

READ AHEAD: PROVERBS 1:10–19

My son, if sinners entice you, don't be persuaded. Proverbs 1:10

When you read this proverb, perhaps you think, "Oh, sinners won't entice me. I don't even hang out with sinners."

But in the Bible, "sinners" refers to anyone who's not actively obeying God. That means the enticing may not come from a drug dealer in the alley or a prostitute on the street corner. It may come from your best friends. Their invitations to sin can be exciting and tempting sometimes, but be careful! They may also lead to great harm.

Many people you know—even those you know closely—make choices without considering God's standards. The book of Proverbs warns, however, that the end result is destruction for those who ignore God in their decisions. And if you allow yourself to be lured into sin with them—just for the thrill of the moment—you also will suffer the consequences.

Don't be fooled! Mistakes made in your youth can haunt you the rest of your life. You may ask for and receive forgiveness for them, but the consequences of your choices can last far into your future. So trust the Holy Spirit to alert you to dangerous invitations. Ask God daily for the strength to say no, even to your best friends.

And one final caution: if you have friends who constantly seek to persuade you into activities that don't honor God, they're not really your friends at all. The Bible calls them sinners. Don't give in to them, and don't spend time with them.

HOW DO YOU KNOW THAT GOD HAS YOUR BEST INTERESTS AT HEART?

READ UP: 2 KINGS 6:8–17 • 1 CORINTHIANS 10:23–33

WHOLE HEARTED

READ AHEAD: PROVERBS 3:5–8

Trust in the Lord with all your heart, and do not rely on your own understanding. Proverbs 3:5

It's one thing to trust God with your mind. It's quite another to trust him with your whole heart. In your mind, for instance, you may be convinced that God is powerful and able to take care of people's needs. But when problems come into your own life, do nagging doubts creep in? Do you wonder if God is really trustworthy? Are you not so sure he'll do what he said he'd do?

A common trap Christians fall into is trusting our own instincts. We face a decision or a problem, and we feel quite capable of handling it our own way. Proverbs urges us, however, not to put trust in our own understanding. We deceive ourselves if we think we're smart enough to make the right choices apart from God.

You've probably heard someone say: "God gave us brains, didn't he? He must want us to figure this out for ourselves." Actually, God gave us his Holy Spirit to guide and teach us. He also gave us the Bible, other Christians, and access to him through prayer. Considering these provisions, there is no need to live without his guidance.

God wants you to rely on his wisdom every day—in all things—not just when you're stumped and can't figure things out on your own. He wants you to trust him above your own best reasoning. Live each day with an attitude of complete trust and obedience, and God will lead you in the right direction every time.

WHY DOES IT SOMETIMES SEEM AS THOUGH GOD IS HIDING HIS ANSWER FROM US?

READ UP: 2 CHRONICLES 16:7–9 • PSALM 40:1–5

LOVE TEST

READ AHEAD: PROVERBS 3:9–10

Honor the Lord with your possessions and with the first produce of your entire harvest. Proverbs 3:9

We love to talk about the things that top our priority lists: sports, clothes, music, movies, computers. These are the things we read about and look up on the Internet. They determine the way we spend our time. We're glad to open up our wallets for something important to us—not because we have to, but because we want to.

Solomon understood this. That's why he said that a good test of our love for God is how well we honor him with our money, not just with our words and our Bible reading.

Some people give to God from whatever they have left over at the end of their paycheck or allowance. They pay for their necessities, pursue their hobbies, and shell out for entertainment. Then if there's anything left over, they give a token offering to God.

But for the person who loves God above everything else, payday is a time to think first about what she can give to God's work. She doesn't begrudge parting with her hard-earned money, because she understands that it came from God in the first place. God provides for her needs and then blesses her beyond that.

Solomon knew a thing or two about God's generosity. No matter how extravagant Solomon's offerings were, he received even more blessings in return. In fact, he became the wealthiest king ever to rule Israel. This proverb was his personal testimony about the blessings that come from honoring God with possessions. It can be the same with you.

WHAT DOES THE WAY YOU SPEND YOUR MONEY SAY ABOUT YOUR DEVOTION TO GOD?

READ UP: MALACHI 3:8–12 • 2 CORINTHIANS 9:6–8

WHY ME?

READ AHEAD: PROVERBS 3:11-12

The Lord disciplines the one He loves, just as a father, the son he delights in. Proverbs 3:12

Do you know God loves you? Do you really know it? You no doubt enjoy God's expressions of love, such as his forgiveness and his blessings.

There are times, though, when God demonstrates his love by disciplining you. He may do this by allowing you to go through a tough time. Don't get angry when God does this. Don't assume he doesn't love you.

The fact that he's disciplining you is actually proof of his love. Because he has perfect knowledge of the future, knows the dangers you face, and wants to build a strong character in you that will benefit you throughout life, he will discipline you to protect you from harm.

Perhaps, for example, you're spending time with the wrong kind of friends. You may be unaware of the effect they're having on you. But God knows the potential for pain and suffering these friendships hold. If you ignore his warnings, he will discipline you. It may not be severe at first, but if you refuse to change, his discipline can become increasingly painful.

There are many areas in your life where you might experience God's discipline: your habits, your attitudes, your relationships, or the entertainment you pursue. Whatever it is that he's cautioning you about, pay attention! He is disciplining you because he loves you . . . and because he'll settle for nothing less than his best for your life.

HOW DO YOU TYPICALLY RESPOND TO THOSE WHO DISCIPLINE YOU?

READ UP: DEUTERONOMY 8:1-5 • HEBREWS 12:5-13

ONE PASSIONATE PURSUIT

READ AHEAD: PROVERBS 4:3–9

Wisdom is supreme—so get wisdom. And whatever else you get, get understanding. Proverbs 4:7

Some people assume that by the time a person gets old, wisdom just automatically happens. But that's a myth. Wisdom is a choice. Yes, some older people are wise, but not just because they have gray hair. People become wise by spending their years walking closely with God, actively pursuing him, paying the price for wisdom, building God's standards into their lives so they can honor him in everything they do.

How, then, can you obtain wisdom?

• *Study God's Word.* The book of Proverbs is a great place to start, but the entire Bible teaches you about godly wisdom. Read your Bible. Learn from the successes (and the failures) of those you read about in the Scriptures.

• *Ask questions.* God is not intimidated by your questions. He welcomes them if you ask them in humility, out of a desire to know him.

• *Be teachable.* Don't be overly sensitive when someone shares a concern he has about you. Listen to his feedback to see if God is teaching you a valuable life lesson through his honest words. We all like praise. No one enjoys being criticized. But we often learn the most from our mistakes.

The direction your life takes will be a result of the choices you make. Choose to go after wisdom. Pursue it with all your energy, and hold on to it. It will enrich your life!

WHAT'S INVOLVED IN WISDOM?
HOW DO YOU KNOW IT WHEN YOU SEE IT?

READ UP: ISAIAH 11:1–5 • MATTHEW 13:44–46

ON GUARD

READ AHEAD: PROVERBS 4:20–27

Guard your heart above all else, for it is the source of life.
Proverbs 4:23

The Bible says it's the heart—not the mind—where our values are kept and our decisions are made.

The world encourages us to develop our minds, the center of our intellect. Some people train their brains to do amazing things. They memorize volumes of information and grasp profound concepts.

Sadly, however, people often neglect their hearts. Some who have the highest IQs don't have good hearts to match. Some of the world's smartest people have destroyed themselves by their own bad decisions. Although they had intelligence, they never cultivated God's values. That's because intelligence comes much more easily than good character. Smart people without morals or integrity are dangerous to be around.

But if you want your life to be filled with the blessings of God, don't neglect your heart. Your problem may not be that you don't have enough knowledge. It may be that your heart is simply not inclined to do what you already know to do!

According to the Bible, the heart includes your emotions and will. It represents who you really are. Your heart is where the great battles and decisions of life are won or lost.

Guard your heart so you are always ready to do what you know is right. Be sure to spend at least as much time developing your heart as you spend developing your mind.

WHAT'S THE POINT, THEN, OF TRYING TO SHARPEN OUR MINDS AND GROW OUR INTELLIGENCE?

READ UP: EZEKIEL 36:24–30 • LUKE 6:43–45

WHAT GOD SEES

READ AHEAD: PROVERBS 5:20–23

A man's ways are before the Lord's eyes, and He considers all his paths. Proverbs 5:21

There's no point in pretending with God! We have no secrets that we keep from him. He knows everything we think, say, and do.

Yes, you can often keep things from your teachers, your parents, and your friends. They can't read your thoughts, so you can hide your actions from them. You may be putting on an act that fools everyone you meet (or at least you think it does). At times, you may even try comforting yourself with the thought: "Thank goodness no one knows what I'm really like. What a relief no one knows what I'm thinking or feeling."

Don't count on it! If you're holding on to secret sin, God sees it. It's no use trying to rationalize why you're doing it, because he knows your motives, as well.

Thankfully, this great truth of Scripture can also work to your advantage. It can be so greatly comforting to know God is always watching over you to protect and guide you. But if your heart is bent on rebellion and disobedience, it can be troubling to know that he clearly sees everything you're doing at all times.

The next time you're considering something that you know isn't right, remember that you have an audience. Before you do something you suspect is wrong, ask yourself: "Do I want God to watch me doing this?"

He is watching, you know.

WHAT COULD YOU DO TO MAKE THIS TRUTH A BLESSING RATHER THAN A BURDEN?

READ UP: JEREMIAH 32:17–19 • HEBREWS 4:12–13

BORROWING TROUBLE

READ AHEAD: PROVERBS 6:1–5

If you have put up security for your neighbor or entered into an agreement with a stranger, you have been trapped. Proverbs 6:1-2

Do friends ever pressure you to fulfill their obligations for them? Don't do it. When someone makes a promise, he must carry it out himself.

For example, if a friend asks you to bail her out of a financial commitment she's made, graciously decline. If a classmate or coworker agrees to a large project, then tries to pass the work off onto you, kindly but firmly refuse.

You just have to be careful in the way you commit yourself, or you'll become so busy meeting the obligations of others, you'll have no time, energy, or money left to keep your own commitments.

Does this sound like an unkind way to treat other people? It's actually very biblical and wise. Many young lives have been severely restricted because of overcommitment. Rather than being free to obey whatever God asks them to do, they find themselves shackled by the careless debts of others.

This doesn't mean you should be unkind or unhelpful to others. But you must allow them to face the responsibility for their own actions. Even the closest friendships have been destroyed because of bad debts and foolish commitments.

Don't let yourself be pressured into doing something out of guilt, for guilt is not the basis for true friendship. Be a person who keeps your own promises, but not those that belong to someone else.

WHERE DO YOU DRAW THE LINE? WHEN IS HELPING NO LONGER A HELP TO SOMEONE?

READ UP: GALATIANS 6:3–5 • 1 THESSALONIANS 4:9–12

THE LAZY LIFE

READ AHEAD: PROVERBS 6:6–11

A little sleep, a little slumber, a little folding of the arms to rest, and your poverty will come on you like a robber. Proverbs 6:10–11

Sleep is a good thing, right? To a point, that is. Rest is good, but too much of it robs you of the time for accomplishing anything.

God designed people to need rest only to remain healthy, but some people take this to the extreme! They find a comfort zone and snuggle down into it. They say: "I will not take risks. I won't exert myself. I'll avoid things that make me uncomfortable. I'll try to get by with as little work as possible."

Habits formed now will be hard to break later. If you set a pattern of always taking the easy road, you'll wake up one day to discover your life is empty and you've accomplished nothing of significance. On the other hand, if you begin investing your efforts into things that are worthwhile, your life will be full and productive.

Shortcuts will always be available. Lots of people will encourage you to take the easiest way. But nothing of lasting value was ever accomplished by those who were always looking for a free ride.

The world has been greatly influenced, not by people trying to protect themselves, but by those who jumped in there to do everything God had laid out for them. Many people are unwilling to pay the price necessary for greatness with God. But you? Strive for excellence in everything you do, because you are doing it all for his glory.

HOW DEEPLY HAS LAZINESS WORMED ITS WAY INTO YOUR LIFE?

READ UP: ECCLESIASTES 11:1–10 • COLOSSIANS 3:16–17

SEVEN BAD SINS

READ AHEAD: PROVERBS 6:16–19

Six things the Lord hates; in fact, seven are detestable to him.
Proverbs 6:16

We like to think of God as a loving God and, indeed, he is. But there are several character traits that he detests. All of them are things that harm us as well as others.

• *Pride*. Putting yourself above others and above God is in complete contrast to the humility Jesus showed.

• *Dishonesty*. Lying damages relationships. God is pure truth, and he hates the very thought of falsehood.

• *Violence*. God is the defender of the helpless and the innocent. Those who try to hurt them are his enemies.

• *Premeditated evil*. God scorns the heart that continually comes up with wicked things to do . . . the heart that loves sin more than God.

• *Delighting in sin*. He forbids us from indulging in sinful practices.

• *Careless words*. When we gossip about others or seek to destroy their reputation, we bring God's anger on ourselves.

• *Troublemaking*. God is a God of peace. He detests it when we purposely seek conflict with others.

Take time to reflect on your personality. Are you a liar? A gossip? A troublemaker? Ask God to tell you what he hates about your character, and seek to change those things that are out of line with his will.

HOW CAN YOU LEARN TO HATE SIN WITHOUT HATING PEOPLE?

READ UP: PSALM 36:1–4 • PSALM 101:2–4

66

MOMS AND DADS

READ AHEAD: PROVERBS 6:20–23

Keep your father's command, and don't reject your mother's teaching. Proverbs 6:20

If you're like most young people, you'll reach a point in life when parental advice is the last thing you want to hear! After all, your parents grew up in a different world. They didn't face the same problems young people face today. Times have changed.

Some of that is undoubtedly true. Nevertheless, some things never change. It was God's idea that wisdom gained by one generation be passed down to the next.

Each generation faces new opportunities and new challenges, yet the truths found in Scripture remain relevant through the centuries. That's why God instructs the young to heed the wisdom found in his Word—wisdom that is passed down from those who are more mature in their faith.

Perhaps your parents are not Christians, though. Even if they are, perhaps they haven't lived out the teaching of the Scriptures as a model for you. This still doesn't excuse you from being teachable, submitting to them, and learning from other Christians who are older and more familiar with God's Word than you are.

If you're smart, you'll take seriously the wise advice you receive from godly adults. Even if you don't understand it, or you think it doesn't apply to you, there will come a time when you'll face an unexpected situation, and you'll be able to draw on the wisdom that a parent, grandparent, or older Christian shared with you.

HOW DO MOST OF THE PEOPLE YOU HANG AROUND WITH FEEL ABOUT THEIR PARENTS?

READ UP: DEUTERONOMY 11:18–21 • EPHESIANS 6:1–4

TREASURE MAP

READ AHEAD: PROVERBS 7:1–4

My son, obey my words, and treasure my commands.
Proverbs 7:1

Sometimes life seems shrouded by doubts and darkness. Worries and uncertainties loom large, like monsters in the closet. Problems pop up, and you can't see your way around them.

For non-Christians, this is the reality of life. Without a relationship with Jesus, they have good reason for their feelings of hopelessness and despair. But Christians don't have to live in the dark. God has given us a lamp. His Word lights the way and shows us where he wants us to go. God has placed his eternal wisdom in the Bible, making it available to anyone who wants to know it.

But his Word is not useful to you if it sits on a shelf in your room. When you read your Bible and memorize verses of Scripture, you are writing them "on the tablet of your heart" (verse 3). Later, when you face temptation, or when you're making an important decision, the Holy Spirit will remind you of Scriptures that apply to your situation.

Don't just scan your Bible quickly each day and then put it away until the next. As you read, ask God to show you a verse that will be important for you to remember. Mark it in your Bible. You may even want to write it down and memorize it.

Filling your mind with God's Word will prepare you for the next dark place you come across.

WHAT MAKES GOD'S TRUTH THE ULTIMATE AUTHORITY ON EVERYTHING?

READ UP: PSALM 19:7–11 • 2 TIMOTHY 3:16–17

YOU NEED TO KNOW

READ AHEAD: PROVERBS 9:7–9

Don't rebuke a mocker, or he will hate you; rebuke a wise man, and he will love you. Proverbs 9:8

One of the ways to tell whether someone is a wise person or a fool is to measure the way he or she responds to advice. Fools don't want to learn. They have no desire to gain wisdom. Wise people, however, treasure good advice, even when it hurts.

Suppose you have a friend who's making some bad choices that you know will lead to trouble. If you point out his sin and try to help him, he will react in one of two ways: anger or acceptance.

• *Anger.* A fool will be more upset at you for pointing out his failings than he will be at himself for having behaved like a fool. He'd rather end his friendship with you than accept your correction. That's why it takes wisdom to recognize when (or when not) to give advice to someone. Wisdom will sometimes guide you to say nothing rather than offend a fool.

• *Acceptance.* A wise person, on the other hand, will welcome your input and thank you for having the courage to correct him. Wise people readily accept good counsel. They have teachable spirits because they want to become wiser still.

Be discerning. Know the difference between a wise person and a fool. Give advice to wise people, but avoid fools. In the long run, it will save you a lot of grief, and it will win you the friendship of wise people.

WHAT HELPS YOU DETERMINE IF YOUR MOTIVE IS TO HELP SOMEONE OR TO VENT YOUR FRUSTRATIONS?

READ UP: 2 SAMUEL 12:1–13 • GALATIANS 4:15–20

GOOD KIDS

READ AHEAD: PROVERBS 10:1-3

A wise son brings joy to his father, but a foolish son, heartache to his mother. Proverbs 10:1

The sad thing about rebellious children is that they cause so much sorrow to the very people who have pleaded with them to be wise. Sin, by its very nature, brings heartache not only to the sinner but also to many other people. The consequences of sin are seldom limited to the one who does the sinning.

The young woman, for example, who is determined to give her body away ends up with an unwanted pregnancy that becomes her parents' burden also. The young man who gets expelled from school stains the reputation of his family. The reason these children are called foolish is because they are blind to the grief and pain they cause to those who love them.

But some children bring joy to their parents, listening to them even when they disagree with them. The wise daughter understands that her parents are motivated by love for her when they caution her to treat her body with respect. The wise son accepts the hard-earned wisdom of his parents and successfully steers his life through difficult choices. Wise children bring honor to their family by the choices they make.

Into which category do you fall? Do you bring joy to your parents? Do you realize the pain your sins can cause them? Perhaps you need to ask your family's forgiveness and begin honoring them today.

WHY DID GOD CREATE US WITH THE ABILITY TO BE AFFECTED BY OTHERS' LIVES?

READ UP: 1 SAMUEL 2:12-26 • COLOSSIANS 3:20-21

EXTRA EFFORT

READ AHEAD: PROVERBS 10:4–5

Idle hands make one poor, but diligent hands bring riches.
Proverbs 10:4

Does it seem out of place for the Bible to teach us how to pursue wealth? It clearly states that "diligent hands bring riches." But this proverb is not just about money. It's about hard work, about diligence and honesty.

Working hard does indeed pay off, not just financially but also by building good character. Staying with a job rather than taking shortcuts produces perseverance. It teaches us to be unselfish. We learn to take pride in a job well done. It also means we can find satisfaction in looking back over the day, the week, or the year—even over a lifetime—and seeing how much we've accomplished.

Lazy people are always trying to avoid work. In fact, they sometimes spend more energy avoiding work than they would if they'd have just done the job in the first place!

They have the misguided attitude that the world owes them something. They're always being cared for and rescued by others. They're takers rather than givers, not bothered by the fact that others are working hard while they're taking it easy.

Is this something you struggle with in your life? If you're trying to figure out shortcuts to get where you want to go, stop your daydreaming and get to work. You stand to gain much more by putting in the necessary effort than by looking for a free ride. As the Bible says, hard work pays off—in many ways.

WHAT'S THE LAZINESS FACTOR OF THE PEOPLE YOU KNOW BEST?

READ UP: NEHEMIAH 4:1–6 • ROMANS 13:11–14

WHAT'S YOUR REPUTATION?

READ AHEAD: PROVERBS 10:6-7

The remembrance of the righteous is a blessing, but the name of the wicked will rot. Proverbs 10:7

How would you like to be remembered? When people hear your name, what mental image would you like them to have of you?

If you live a righteous life—choosing to honor God with what you say and do—you will create a legacy of blessing others. People will know they can trust you. They will be better people because of your friendship. If God leads you to move somewhere else, those you leave behind will remember you fondly as someone whom God used to bless them. Over a lifetime there will be many whose lives were richer because you were a part of it.

On the other hand, if you're not careful with sin in your life, you will leave a far different impression on people. If you are selfish, egotistical, vindictive, or unreliable in your relationships, a day will come when you discover you have a reputation you never wanted. When your name is mentioned, people will immediately have negative thoughts about you. People will not want to be around you. They will warn others about you. You will not be trusted.

Sadly, some people never realize that the reason others avoid them or don't trust them is because they've allowed sinful behavior to tarnish their reputation. Now is a good time to decide how you'd like to be remembered, and to make a conscious choice to develop a good reputation.

HOW BADLY WOULD MOST PEOPLE LIKE A DIFFERENT REPUTATION THAN THE ONE THEY HAVE?

READ UP: LUKE 2:51-52 • 1 THESSALONIANS 1:2-10

A SAFE PLACE

READ AHEAD: PROVERBS 10:8–9

The one who lives with integrity lives securely. Proverbs 10:9

Life is full of surprises. We can never be absolutely sure what awaits us around the corner. Yet God says we can be secure, unafraid of the little things that can jump up and bite us.

The key to our security is our integrity.

Integrity means being blameless, having no hypocrisy, being honest in every aspect of our lives, and being genuine all the time. Your integrity is revealed when you respond appropriately to something, even though you didn't have time to plan your actions in advance. You see it in people whose lives line up with what they say they believe. It means doing the right thing . . . even when no one is watching.

It's like driving a car. You'll be more secure when you obey traffic laws than when you break them. If you exceed the speed limit, you won't feel secure because you'll be on the lookout for flashing lights. You'll know that much is at stake if you're caught.

You'll have far more peace of mind if you don't have to worry about being found out. You won't have to worry about people discovering what you've done, because you'll have nothing to hide from them. This gives you tremendous freedom!

God's advice to you is to live with integrity, enjoying the freedom that comes from a life that pleases God all day long.

IF WE WANT TO BE WHOLE PEOPLE (GENUINE AND TRUSTWORTHY) WHY DON'T WE DO IT?

READ UP: JOB 27:1–6 • PSALM 86:11–13

NICE TO SEE YOU

READ AHEAD: PROVERBS 10:10–11

The mouth of the righteous is a fountain of life.
Proverbs 10:11

Some people are so easy to be around. They're happy and positive about life. They don't become angry easily. They make you feel good about yourself. They don't criticize you or offend you with careless comments. They don't gossip or say false things about you or others.

You feel safe being around them because you know they care about you. When you're with them, they give you life.

Others, though, seem to have an angry or violent streak in them. They hurt you with their words. There's a real harshness about them. They're often negative and use their words as weapons. They take pleasure in ridiculing others. When you're with them, they often laugh at other people (and you suspect they make fun of you, too, when you're not there!). When you're around people like this, you feel life draining from you.

What kind of person are you? Do you bring out the best in others? Do people seem drawn to you, or do they avoid spending time with you? Do people know you care about them, or are they right in assuming you don't?

You have the opportunity to be a source of life to those around you. Strive to be an encouragement to others. There are far too few people like this in the world . . . and far too many who are desperately looking to be refreshed.

WHAT KEEPS PEOPLE FROM PAYING ATTENTION TO OTHERS?

READ UP: 2 SAMUEL 9:1–13 • 2 CORINTHIANS 2:14–17

LET'S BE FRIENDS

READ AHEAD: PROVERBS 10:12-17

Hatred stirs up conflicts, but love covers all offenses.
Proverbs 10:12

Nothing compares to the power of love in bringing healing to someone who has sinned. God, for example, chose to redeem a sinful world, not by punishing us, but by loving us and sending his Son to die for us.

Don't underestimate how much your love can help someone who is carrying a burden of sin. When a friend is caught in sin, don't withdraw and tell everyone what your friend has done. Instead, find ways to restore him. Help him be reconciled with those he has offended. Encourage him to lean on the incredible love of God.

Has someone sinned against you? How are you going to respond? Will you refuse to forgive? Will you strike back in anger? Will you break off your friendship? Will you continue to bring up the offense?

Love doesn't do that. Love forgives. Love doesn't hold on to a grudge or continue to make the person feel guilty. Love gives another chance. Love assumes the best of those who sin against you. Genuine love forgives *many* sins, not just the first one. There should be no limit to your forgiveness.

If you have friends who are suffering from the consequences of their sins, why not reach out in love today to help bring them healing? God will take care of disciplining them. He asks you simply to love the people around you.

WHAT'S THE FIRST THING YOU TYPICALLY DO WHEN SOMEONE MISTREATS YOU?

READ UP: MATTHEW 18:21-35 • COLOSSIANS 3:12-15

WHAT YOU SAID

READ AHEAD: PROVERBS 10:18–21

When there are many words, sin is unavoidable, but the one who controls his lips is wise. Proverbs 10:19

Every time you speak, your words have the potential either to bring joy to others or to cause great pain.

Words of encouragement don't always come easily. Building up others requires that we first think about what they need to hear, and then allow the Holy Spirit time to give us the words he wants us to say. This requires setting aside the desire to do all the talking, focusing our attention instead on the other person. It means resisting the urge to interrupt every time we think of something to say.

A fool, on the other hand, doesn't think before speaking. A fool is never concerned about saying the right thing at the right time. Opportunities to say an encouraging word are often lost, because the fool is unprepared and preoccupied with selfish thoughts. Some of the deepest hurts people carry throughout life have come from careless words spoken to them by a fool.

Have you missed opportunities to bless others because you were too busy talking to listen to them? Are you in the habit of blurting out comments without thinking of the potential damage your words could cause?

Commit yourself to becoming a wise person whose words bring comfort and encouragement. Ask questions, listen more, and talk less. You'll be pleased with the results, and so will those around you.

IF YOU SPEAK THE TRUTH, BUT SAY IT IN THE WRONG WAY, WHAT KIND OF DAMAGE CAN THAT DO?

READ UP: PSALM 73:13–17 • JAMES 3:7–12

WHAT'S THE MATTER?

READ AHEAD: PROVERBS 12:19–26

Anxiety in a man's heart weighs it down, but a good word cheers it up. Proverbs 12:25

How well do you know your friends? Can you tell when something is bothering them, before they even say a word? Does their face give them away?

If you know your friends well enough, you should be able to tell by their behavior when their hearts are heavy, because their anxiety will affect the way they view everything. They won't enjoy the good things that are happening around them. Everything will look dark to them. They might act moody or critical.

When this happens, don't jump to conclusions. They might not even be aware that their anxiety is affecting the way they treat you. Rather than striking back, ask God to help you show kindness toward your friend. It could be that God has chosen you to deliver a message of encouragement exactly when your friend needs it most.

If this is so, the Holy Spirit will prompt you to know what to say. He may give you a specific Bible verse to share, or he may lead you just to listen so your friend can talk about what's worrying her. The important thing is that you are sensitive to what is happening in your friend's life, and that you're prepared to be God's instrument of encouragement.

In the same way, when *your* heart is anxious about something, listen carefully for God's special message for you. Your problems are never too small for him to notice or too personal for him to become involved.

WHAT CAUSES YOU AND YOUR FRIENDS THE MOST ANXIETY TODAY?

READ UP: PSALM 73:21–28 • 1 PETER 5:6–7

THE RAW TRUTH

READ AHEAD: PROVERBS 12:27–28

A lazy man doesn't roast his game, but to a diligent man, his wealth is precious. Proverbs 12:27

Do you know what this verse is really saying? It says a lazy person doesn't even bother to cook his meat. He eats it raw!

Disgusting, isn't it?

Some things only come through hard work. God has so much he wants to do in your life, he doesn't want you to sleep through any of it. But some opportunities come only once, and if you're too slow to respond or too careless to recognize them, you'll miss out.

That's why, even though we sometimes think of laziness as being more of a personality trait or weakness, the Bible calls it a sin. Nothing less.

God has placed people around you who need you to be purposeful in the way you live. Those who are younger than you don't know how to live as Christ desires. You can be their model. Many people your age are desperate for a word of encouragement. You can be their friend. There are people of all ages around you who need to experience the love of Christ. You can give it to them. You cannot allow God to use your life to the maximum and be lazy at the same time. It's impossible.

Jesus said he came to give you life to the fullest, the best life there is! But the trap of laziness will rob you of the great things he has to offer. Seek diligently after righteousness, and you'll experience life the way God intends for you to experience it.

WHAT HAVE YOU EVER MISSED BECAUSE YOU WEREN'T PAYING ATTENTION OR HAD QUIT TRYING?

READ UP: MATTHEW 25:1–13 • LUKE 12:35–40

SPOKE TOO SOON

READ AHEAD: PROVERBS 13:1–5

The one who guards his mouth protects his life; the one who opens his lips invites his own ruin. Proverbs 13:3

Our generation can hardly tolerate quiet. We'd rather fill the air with foolishness than endure an awkward silence.

That's why, far too often, we speak first and think later. We assume that the only words worth listening to are the ones coming out of our own mouths. So rather than really listening to our friends, we use their words as springboards to launch our own opinions.

Even our best intentions can be sabotaged if we speak up too quickly. For example, if a friend shares a problem, and we blurt out bad advice without even thinking about the implications, we can cause more harm than good. Rarely do we regret taking the time to think before we speak, but how often do we long to take back something we said on the spur of the moment?

Careless words, tossed out without thinking, possess more power than we might think. They have the power to hurt others or embarrass them. They're like feathers shaken into the wind, impossible to retrieve once the wind has carried them away. That's how impossible it is to recover even a single hurtful word once it has left our mouths.

You do, however, have protection from regretting what you say. It's called silence. When you're tempted to speak without thinking or to say something unkind, it's better to say nothing at all. Silence is never as awkward as rashly spoken words.

WHEN IS IT BEST TO BE SILENT, AND WHEN IS IT BEST TO SPEAK UP?

READ UP: MARK 15:1–5 • JAMES 4:7–12

ONE SURE INVESTMENT

READ AHEAD: PROVERBS 13:6–12

Delayed hope makes the heart sick, but fulfilled desire is a tree of life. Proverbs 13:12

If you're counting on people to fulfill your dreams, you're setting yourself up for disappointment. People make lots of promises, but not all of them come to pass. Even those with the best intentions can't always come through when it counts.

But God will.

You have certain things you hope for. You may spend great amounts of time thinking about and wishing for them. Maybe it's a relationship you hope will improve. Perhaps it's a job or career you desire. The possibilities are limitless for what you might be anticipating.

It's vitally important, however, that you put your hope in the right place. Don't expect your parents, your friends, your boyfriend or girlfriend, or your future husband or wife to satisfy your inner longing for contentment. They can't do it. Neither can money or a certain social status.

There's only one person who will never fail you when you place your hope in him, and that's God. Your only guarantee against disappointment is to put your hope in him.

If you've been quick to take your longings to other people but slow to take them to God, you've been shortchanging yourself. Don't ask others to try to fill the gaps in your soul that only God can fill. Put your hope in him, because he delivers on every promise he makes.

WHY ARE WE UNABLE TO MEET OTHER PEOPLE'S NEEDS FULLY, EVEN IF WE REALLY WANT TO?

READ UP: PSALM 33:16–22 • HEBREWS 6:13–20

I HEAR YOU

READ AHEAD: PROVERBS 13:13–18

Poverty and disgrace come to those who ignore instruction, but the one who accepts rebuke will be honored. Proverbs 13:18

It's safe to assume that you're not perfect. In fact, it's probably safe to say that you're *far* from perfect—like all of us are. We're all in need of all the help we can get! The sooner we realize this, the better off we'll be.

That's because God is not satisfied for us to remain spiritual babies. He wants each of us to become spiritually mature. To bring this maturity about, therefore, he gives us lots of opportunities to grow . . . by placing people in our lives to guide and assist us.

But here's the question: will we (or will we not) take advantage of these opportunities? Our pride and insecurity often prevent us from learning the lessons we need to learn, even though refusing to take correction is as foolish as an athlete who refuses to listen to her coach.

God has placed people in your life who are wiser than you are, people who care about you. If you reject their wise counsel because you feel it jeopardizes your self-worth, you'll never mature as God desires. If you're smart, however, you'll not only *listen* to good advice, you'll also *seek it out*. Spending even a few minutes listening to wise counsel from people you respect could save you years of future grief!

The choice is yours. You can try figuring things out on your own, or you can trust that those whom God has placed in authority over you usually know what's best for you.

WHAT'S SOME OF THE BEST ADVICE YOU EVER GOT, ALTHOUGH YOU DIDN'T THINK SO AT THE TIME?

READ UP: GALATIANS 2:11–14 • 2 PETER 1:12–15

BEST FRIENDS

READ AHEAD: PROVERBS 13:20–21

The one who walks with the wise will become wise, but a companion of fools will suffer harm. Proverbs 13:20

Have you ever noticed how people and their dogs grow to look alike over the years? Maybe that's a myth, but it is true that you're shaped by the company you keep. If you spend time with wise people, you'll grow in wisdom. If you stick around fools, their foolishness will rub off on you.

Choosing your friends shouldn't be a haphazard venture, because they have a tremendous influence on your life. If you spend a lot of time with a gossip, it'll be hard to resist falling into the same habit. If your friend has a critical spirit, you may find yourself growing judgmental as well.

This is not to say you need to eliminate all imperfect people from your social circle. It does mean, however, that you should choose friends who are striving to honor God with their lives. If your friend has no concern for Christian values, it will be an uphill battle to stay in the friendship and maintain your own integrity.

Actively seek out friends who will affect your character in positive ways. These people will challenge you to grow as a Christian, and you will enjoy being around them. At the same time, be sure you're a good influence on your friends. They should be better people because they know you.

Take a few minutes to evaluate your friendships. Are they affecting you in ways you don't want?

WHAT DO YOU DO WHEN YOUR FRIENDS AND YOUR PARENTS SAY TWO DIFFERENT THINGS?

READ UP: DANIEL 3:1–18 • EPHESIANS 5:15–21

OWNING UP

READ AHEAD: PROVERBS 14:8–12

Fools mock at making restitution, but there is goodwill among the upright. Proverbs 14:9

One of the biggest mistakes Christians make is to underestimate the power of sin. We don't like to admit when we sin, because then we have to make amends for it or change our behavior. So we rationalize that we haven't really sinned at all.

• *First, we find a better name for it.* Sin sounds so old-fashioned. So harsh. Let's call it a "mistake" or a "habit" or a "lapse in judgment." That sounds better.

• *Next, we build a case to explain why we did it.* "Everyone else was doing it." "I didn't think anyone would get hurt." "It wasn't my fault."

• *Finally, we de-emphasize the fallout.* "People are too uptight these days." "They need to stop being so sensitive."

It comes down to a control issue. We don't like being told what to do. We want the freedom to make our own choices. But we fail to understand one thing: We don't control sin. Sin controls us.

Sin is any attitude or behavior that goes against God's desires. He wants us to be free from the guilt, shame, and consequences of sin. But as long as we refuse to take sin seriously, we'll never experience life the way God desires.

Don't be afraid to see sin for what it is. Don't allow a distorted view of sin to rob you of the life God intends for you. Ask God to tell you how you can make amends.

WHAT SINS IN YOUR LIFE NEED TO BE EXPOSED FOR WHAT THEY ARE?

READ UP: ROMANS 6:16–23 • GALATIANS 6:7–8

I'LL DO BETTER

READ AHEAD: PROVERBS 14:14–16

The disloyal will get what their conduct deserves, and a good man what his deeds deserve. Proverbs 14:14

Christians are delighted whenever someone rededicates her life to God. People regularly stand up before the church and share a renewed resolve to start living for Christ. We all smile and nod our approval.

Sounds good, doesn't it? So what's the problem?

The problem is: promises are easily made and easily broken. God isn't satisfied with promises. He's satisfied with obedience. Disobeying God is a serious matter. That's why, when someone realizes he has been living in sin . . .

- It's time for grieving, not rejoicing.
- It's time for brokenness, not celebration.
- It's time for repentance, not rededication.

God isn't looking for another promise. He's looking for repentance. And the evidence of repentance is a changed life.

Sometimes we think if we make enough promises in front of enough people, we'll finally be able to live an obedient life. We dismiss our sin with a promise to do better next time. We're in such a hurry to get on with it that we never stop to consider what we've done and to ask God's forgiveness.

Don't be fooled into believing God is pleased with the promises you make. He's only pleased with the ones you keep.

WHAT STANDS BETWEEN YOU AND KEEPING YOUR PROMISES?

READ UP: 1 SAMUEL 15:17–22 • PSALM 119:9–16

84

BEFORE YOU BLOW UP

READ AHEAD: PROVERBS 14:17-18

A quick-tempered man acts foolishly, and a man who schemes is hated. Proverbs 14:17

It's a mark of maturity when you don't allow your feelings to control your actions. That's not to say self-control comes automatically with age. Many adults live with deep regret for things they've said and done in the heat of emotion. Self-control is a spiritual thing, not an age thing. It's a sign of *spiritual* maturity, not *physical* maturity.

Life is full of emotionally charged events. Things happen every day that can send you over the edge if you let them. In fact, you have little control over much of what happens to you. Unless you find yourself a nice little cabin in the woods and become a hermit, people and circumstances can and will affect your life.

The question is: how are you going to respond? That's something you *can* control. Jesus had every reason in the world to strike back in anger at those who hurt him, but he chose to forgive them instead.

Never make excuses for a quick temper. Eliminate phrases like these from your vocabulary: "I was tired." "I was hurt." "I was under a lot of stress." "You pushed me too far!" "Redheads are *supposed* to be hotheads!" "I'm just a passionate person!"

Self-control is one of the fruits of the Spirit—a sign of the Holy Spirit's working in your life. Since Christ lives within you, you have the ability to respond in love rather than react in anger. Ask God to show you how.

HOW DO YOU SPOT YOUR BOILING POINTS BEFORE YOU'VE ALREADY BOILED OVER?

READ UP: EPHESIANS 4:25-32 • JAMES 1:19-21

UNDER THE SURFACE

READ AHEAD: PROVERBS 16:1–3

All a man's ways seem right in his own eyes, but the Lord weighs the motives. Proverbs 16:2

Is the right thing still the right thing if it's done for the wrong reason?

What if you go to church just to please your parents instead of going to please God? What if you share a prayer request about your friend's problem, but what you're really doing is spreading gossip? What if you do good things for others, but only because it makes them think better of you?

It's possible to do all the right things, but with all the wrong motives.

A person's motives say a lot! When police try to solve a crime, *motive* is one of the most important pieces of the puzzle. Amazingly, though, we're often the worst judges of our own motives. We live our Christian lives, rarely examining why we do what we do. We go through the motions, even though our heart is far from the Lord.

God wants us to live out our faith purposefully. He wants us to do what we do for the right reason—because we love him.

Do you want to grow as a Christian? Then invite God to probe deeply into your character and show you why you do what you do. If you don't like what you see, that's your opportunity for growth, an open window to make a deep difference in your character. Ask him to help you do the right thing for the right reason, and your faith will become much more meaningful to you!

WHY ARE APPEARANCES SUCH A MOTIVATOR IN OUR LIVES?

READ UP: MATTHEW 23:23–28 • JAMES 4:1–3

FALSE ADVERTISING

READ AHEAD: PROVERBS 20:1-2

Wine is a mocker, beer is a brawler, and whoever staggers because of them is not wise. Proverbs 20:1

If all the advice in the book of Proverbs could be boiled down to one sentence, it might read something like this: "Don't believe everything you hear."

Alcohol should be included as one of those things. To hear the world talk, drinking actually enhances your life. It relaxes you and loosens you up so you can have a good time. The commercials reveal all the great things that will happen to you as long as you choose the right beer: cars, sports, travel, romance, adventure, excitement, good friends, good times, great music—whatever you need to make you happy.

But have you heard the rest of the story? Alcohol will play you for a fool. It will destroy your perspective. It will dull your senses, causing you to do foolish and dangerous things. It will remove your inhibitions, making you say and do things you'll regret. Alcohol has caused more heartache than the world is willing to admit: broken hearts and broken homes, lost dreams and lost hopes, despair and even death.

The world says, "Go ahead, it won't hurt you." But when all is said and done and your self-respect has vanished, the writer of Proverbs says alcohol stands back and laughs at you. (The commercials forget to mention that part.)

If you're trusting the world to tell you where to find joy, you're heading for disappointment. Go to God. He'll tell you the whole story.

WHAT THINGS ARE YOU PRESSURED TO BE TOLERANT ABOUT, EVEN IF YOU DON'T DO THEM YOURSELF?

READ UP: GALATIANS 1:6-9 • TITUS 3:3-11

THE BEST COMEBACK

READ AHEAD: PROVERBS 20:3–4

It is honorable for a man to resolve a dispute, but any fool can get himself into a quarrel. Proverbs 20:3

Conflict has been part of the human condition since Cain killed Abel in a fit of jealousy. Whether it's on a grand scale (like a world war) or a smaller scale (like an argument between siblings), conflict has been a part of life throughout human history.

Some people just seem to have a knack for making us angry. They know exactly which buttons to push to get us to lose our cool. It's not as though we're looking for trouble. These people just seem to stir up anger from deep within us.

The Bible calls people like this "fools." But guess what? The Bible says we're fools, too, if we quarrel with them. Any fool can pick a fight, but it takes a lot more character to avoid one . . . or better yet, to resolve one.

It's ingrained in us to fight back when someone hurts us or to get revenge when someone wrongs us. We even get involved in fights that don't concern us because we can't stand to see wrongs go unpunished. But it takes far more courage to stop a conflict than it does to start one.

As you go about your business today, remember that God hasn't asked you to prove how right you are. He's simply asked you to bring peace, even if it means swallowing hard and backing down when you're right. The sign of true wisdom is the ability to *end* an argument, not the ability to *win* one.

WHAT DOES GOD LOOK FOR IN A PEACEMAKER?

READ UP: GENESIS 33:1–11 • 2 CORINTHIANS 5:18–21

NOT SO FAST

READ AHEAD: PROVERBS 20:5–7

Counsel in a man's heart is deep water; but a man of understanding draws it up. Proverbs 20:5

Discernment is the ability to see past the surface of things. Those who are discerning have sharp insight that allows them to see through people who are trying to deceive or mislead them.

It's unfortunately true—people are out there looking to take advantage of you. This doesn't mean you need to become hardhearted and cynical, always suspecting that everyone is out to get you. At the same time, though, it's vitally important that you're not gullible enough to be taken in by the schemes of cunning people.

If someone is asking you to do something you know is wrong, don't be swayed—no matter how convincing the argument or how appealing the person is. Always weigh what others tell you against God's Word, and match their arguments up with biblical principles you know are true. When in doubt, seek the advice of a Christian you respect.

But above all, trust God to guide you. He sees what people plot in their hearts, and he can protect you. He has given you his Holy Spirit to alert you to things that are false. If you have any doubt at all about someone's motives, guard your heart and take your concerns to God.

Are people asking you to do something you're not sure about? Don't proceed until God has given you the assurance that it's okay.

WHAT ARE THE FINE LINES BETWEEN BEING GUARDED AND BEING GULLIBLE?

READ UP: 1 CORINTHIANS 2:10–16 • EPHESIANS 4:11–16

SOMETHING FOR NOTHING

READ AHEAD: PROVERBS 20:21-24

An inheritance gained prematurely will not be blessed ultimately.
Proverbs 20:21

What motivates people to gamble or to buy lottery tickets? Some will tell you it's the thrill of the game. Others will say it's just for fun.

The ones who are really honest will tell you the truth: it's an opportunity to get a big return for a little investment. Something for nothing.

Shortcuts to success hold tremendous appeal. In fact, some folks spend more energy on doomed "get-rich-quick" schemes than they would if they simply resigned themselves to working for a living! They're always looking for their big break, the opportunity of a lifetime. As someone has said, though, "Opportunities are usually disguised as hard work, so most people don't recognize them!"

- Are you obsessed with getting things for nothing?
- Do you find it hard to be patient until you can afford something?
- Do you have a tendency to use other people for your own gain?
- Can you persevere with hard work over a long period of time?

Here's a fact of life: things bought without a cost are usually worth exactly what you pay for them. Don't waste your energy looking for shortcuts. Trust God's timing. He'll see that you get what you need when you're ready for it.

WHAT MIGHT BE GOD'S PURPOSE FOR MAKING US WAIT A WHILE FOR OUR SHIP TO COME IN?

READ UP: HEBREWS 11:8-16 • JAMES 5:7-8

A PEEK INSIDE

READ AHEAD: PROVERBS 20:27–30

A person's breath is the lamp of the Lord, searching the innermost parts. Proverbs 20:27

Oxford University in England sells T-shirts that bear this saying:

The more I study, the more I learn,

The more I learn, the more I know,

The more I know, the more I forget,

The more I forget, the less I know,

So why study?

When you put it that way, it's a hard question to answer. This is a pretty good line, too: *The older you get, the more you realize how little you know.*

Believe it or not, as you grow older, you'll realize more and more that you don't really know yourself the way you thought you did. You may have always considered yourself to be a forgiving person. Then someone hurts you, and you discover you're not as forgiving as you thought. You may have always felt like you were easy to get along with, but the comments you hear and the feedback you get are starting to make you wonder.

We don't really know our hearts the way we might think. That's why we need to ask God to show us what we're really like so we can grow and change. God knows everything there is to know about us—both the good and the bad. Ask him to reveal everything you need to know about your character . . . so it can become more like his.

HOW CAN WE POSSIBLY BE SO BLIND TO OURSELVES?

READ UP: JOB 31:35–37 • PSALM 139:23–24

A GOOD NAME

READ AHEAD: PROVERBS 22:1–6

A good name is to be chosen over great wealth; favor is better than silver and gold. Proverbs 22:1

A good name may eventually lead to riches, but riches don't necessarily lead to a good name. A good reputation is a priceless treasure, but you can't buy one. You can't even inherit one from your parents. Sooner or later, your good name will have to be your own.

When the writer of Proverbs talked about the idea of a "good name," he was thinking about integrity—who you are, not what you've got—the kind of reputation that's earned by living your life well, building it over time. So if you want others to trust you, you must first prove you're trustworthy. If you want others to respect you, you must first earn their respect. If you want to have friends, you need to demonstrate a pattern of being a good friend yourself.

Right now, you're in the process of establishing your own reputation. Even as you're getting your education or beginning your career, you're making a name for yourself. Everything you say or do is creating an image in people's minds of what you're like. People are watching you, listening to you, and forming their opinions about what kind of person you are.

Because it takes so long to establish a good name, few things are more foolish than to throw it away. More than that—as believers—we have Christ's name attached to ours. That's why we need to be sure we're representing both names well. Wise people put a lot of stock in a good name.

WHAT HAPPENS TO PEOPLE WHO DON'T KNOW THE VALUE OF A GOOD NAME?

READ UP: JEREMIAH 9:23–24 • 1 PETER 2:11–12

PAY AS YOU GO

READ AHEAD: PROVERBS 22:22-27

If you have no money to pay, even your bed will be taken from under you. Proverbs 22:27

It's foolish to make promises we know we can't keep. That was true when this proverb was written, and it's still true today.

Yet we can be in such a hurry to get what we want, we find ourselves over our heads in debt. We can't stand to wait, so we sign on the dotted line, getting what we want now with a promise to pay later. Then we cross our fingers and hope the money comes in before the bill does!

Even though the book of Proverbs was written thousands of years ago, its advice is still relevant: if you don't have the money up front, don't buy it! Agreeing to make a regular payment, such as a car payment or a house payment, is not foolish, perhaps, as long as your income enables you to make the payments. But agreeing to pay for something when you don't have the money to honor the loan is dishonest and irresponsible. Proverbs warns you never to bind your future with the foolish choices of your past.

Be careful, especially now while you're young, that you don't saddle yourself with debt. Keep yourself free to respond to God's leading.

Wouldn't it be tragic if God called you to seminary or to the mission field, if he suddenly changed the direction you always anticipated you'd go, and you were too shackled with unnecessary debt to obey?

WHAT HAS YOUR OR YOUR FAMILY'S EXPERIENCE WITH DEBT ALREADY TAUGHT YOU?

READ UP: 2 KINGS 4:1-7 • LUKE 7:40-43

GOOD OLD DAYS

READ AHEAD: PROVERBS 22:28

Don't move an ancient property line that your fathers set up.
Proverbs 22:28

In the ancient Middle East, land was a precious commodity. There were no fences in those times to distinguish where one person's property ended and someone else's began. Instead, families would mark their boundaries with stone markers. Even when ownership of the property would be handed down from one generation to the next, the boundaries would remain the same.

But if someone wanted to rob his neighbor, he might move an ancient landmark to give himself more acreage. This was a demonstration of gross disrespect for his neighbor, as well as for his neighbor's ancestors.

The same rule applies today. When you're tempted to do something foolish with your life, keep in mind that your actions will affect other people beside yourself.

It could be that your parents have spent a lifetime establishing a good reputation in your community. Will you tarnish their good name with one careless decision?

While you're young, you won't always understand why your parents or grandparents consider some things important. But it's important to respect their traditions. Think very carefully about what's at stake before you move a boundary stone. There may be very good reasons why certain values and traditions have been passed down from generation to generation. Realize that some boundaries need to be kept where they are.

HOW DO YOU HANDLE THE BALANCING ACT BETWEEN ASKING QUESTIONS AND RESPECTING TRADITIONS?

READ UP: PSALM 78:1–7 • JEREMIAH 6:16–19

GOOD JOB

READ AHEAD: PROVERBS 22:29

Do you see a man skilled in his work? He will stand in the presence of kings. Proverbs 22:29

What kind of mental image does the word *work* conjure up for you?

If you think of it in a negative sense, you'll never work any harder than you must in order to meet the minimum requirement. Your only focus will be on the amount of your paycheck, and you'll work just hard enough to earn the money you need in order to buy something or go somewhere. You'll see work as a necessary evil merely to be endured until quitting time. You'll always try to get the most return for the least effort.

If that's your opinion of work, you still have some growing to do.

The Bible presents work as a positive thing. Regardless of the pay—or whether there's any compensation at all—work is a good thing all by itself. When you do your best at a job—whatever job it is—it does something good for you. But if you put in just enough effort to get by, you'll never become the person God wants you to be.

You may be thinking, "But what about workaholics? They work *too* much, neglecting their health and their families." That's true. You can definitely do too much work. But you can never do too good a job.

No matter what God calls you to do, give it your best effort. Never settle for mediocrity, and establish excellence as your standard. You don't have to work all the time, but never settle for anything less than your best.

WHAT KIND OF WORK GETS THE MOST OUT OF YOU? WHAT DO YOU REALLY ENJOY DOING?

READ UP: ACTS 18:1–3 • 2 THESSALONIANS 3:6–15

HEART TO HEART

READ AHEAD: PROVERBS 23:26–28

My son, give me your heart, and let your eyes observe my ways.
Proverbs 23:26

When we talk about the heart, we're usually referring to our emotions.

Romantically speaking, for example, we feel as though we have little control over what happens to our hearts. We can lose them or give them away. Others can break them or take them from us, as the old country tune says: "You Done Tore Out My Heart and Stomped That Sucker Flat."

But when the *Bible* refers to the heart, it's talking about your whole being, the whole package—not just your emotions, but your mind, your soul, and your will.

So when God asks for your heart, he's asking for everything. When he controls your heart, he has control of everything about you: your hopes and dreams, your thoughts and fears, your priorities and values, your wisdom, your knowledge, all of it. And unlike in romance, you can be sure your heart is always safe with him.

When the Bible talks about relating to other people, it cautions you to "guard your heart" carefully (Proverbs 4:23). But when it talks about relating to God, it says just the opposite. Don't be afraid to trust him with every ounce of your being. You'll only harm yourself by withholding something from God rather than handing over every part of your life to him. If you've been withholding any part of yourself from him, remember this: whatever you give to God is safe with him.

HOW DO YOU "GIVE" GOD YOUR THOUGHTS, YOUR DREAMS, YOUR EMOTIONS, YOUR WILL?

READ UP: JEREMIAH 24:1–7 • HEBREWS 10:19–23

EVIL EYE

READ AHEAD: PROVERBS 24:1–6

Don't envy evil men or desire to be with them, for their hearts plan violence, and their words stir up trouble. Proverbs 24:1–2

What do wicked people look like? Do they dress in black? Do they have shifty eyes? Are they ugly or covered with warts?

What do they act like? Do they prowl around at night? Do they have a sinister laugh? If only they were so easy to recognize!

The truth is, evil people are often attractive and pleasant . . . on the outside, at least. But appearances can be deceiving. No matter how they look or act outwardly, wicked people hide sin and violence in their hearts. Their goal is to cause you harm.

Be careful that you never envy a wicked person. You might find yourself admiring someone who appears successful by the world's standards, but don't be fooled by that. Sometimes, success comes at the expense of truth and goodness. The Bible teaches that, sooner or later, evil people will be exposed for who they are. In the meantime, don't let anyone who is motivated by sin set the direction for your life.

Ask God for the wisdom to discern whether someone is living for God or living for his own desires. If a friend or acquaintance tries to get you to go against what you know God wants for you, stay away from her!

You might conclude that this proverb doesn't apply to you, because you don't know anyone who's wicked. Hopefully, you're right! But ask God to open your eyes . . . just to be sure.

WHAT'S YOUR DEFINITION OF "EVIL"?

READ UP: PSALM 37:1–11 • 2 CORINTHIANS 11:12–15

READY FOR ANYTHING

READ AHEAD: PROVERBS 24:7–10

If you do nothing in a difficult time, your strength is limited.
Proverbs 24:10

If you're hoping for a trouble-free life, you're heading for disappointment. No matter who you are, how nice you are, how wealthy you are, or how attractive you are, you will never escape problems in this life.

Now is the time to prepare your character so you'll be able to handle adversity when it comes.

The most important thing you can do is to spend time with God. He knows what awaits you in life, and he can prepare you for it so you won't crumble when the trials come. The more you grow in your relationship with him, the stronger your character will be, because you'll be more like Christ. The more fully you know God, the more you'll trust him and increase your faith in him. As he consistently helps you every time you experience trouble, you'll expect him to be there for you the next time you have a problem.

What if you've just come through a difficult experience and you collapsed because you weren't strong enough to handle the load? Did you become discouraged? Did you turn your back on your faith? Were you trying to handle the problem on your own strength?

Learn from your mistake. Like a ship captain who realizes his ship has drifted off its path, make a midcourse correction. Get back into your regular times with God. Ask him to strengthen you for the next trial so you'll be able to experience victory in spite of your circumstances.

WHEN DO YOU FIND IT HARDEST TO TRUST GOD? WHEN DO YOU FEEL THE WEAKEST SPIRITUALLY?

READ UP: PSALM 61:1–4 • MARK 14:32–38

IS THAT MY PROBLEM?

READ AHEAD: PROVERBS 24:11–12

Rescue those being taken off to death, and save those stumbling toward slaughter. Proverbs 24:11

There's an enormous difference between your life and that of a non-Christian. Beyond treating others in a basically moral way, non-Christians really only have one responsibility—themselves. Unless they choose otherwise, they're under no obligation to do anything more than just get through life as best they can.

Christians, on the other hand, have a much greater obligation to those around us. We are to share the love of Christ with others.

But that's not always an easy thing to do. Sometimes we're so busy with our own concerns, we don't take time for other people's needs. It's possible to become so preoccupied with ourselves that we don't even notice the hurting person right next to us.

According to this proverb, however, the "I'm too busy" excuse doesn't hold weight with God. If we'll just open our eyes, we'll see the struggling people all around us, headed for disaster unless someone tells them about God's salvation. We might like to think it's none of our business, but God says it is. He has placed us in the midst of a hurting world so we can share Christ's love with those who desperately need it.

Let God lead you out of your comfort zone so you can help someone else. Ask the Holy Spirit to open your ears and your eyes so you can hear God's prompting and see the needs all around you. Make the effort to get involved.

HOW HAVE YOU BEEN IMPACTED BY SOMEONE WHO THOUGHT MORE OF OTHERS THAN HIMSELF?

READ UP: MATTHEW 5:14–16 • ACTS 20:22–27

NO GLOATING ZONE

READ AHEAD: PROVERBS 24:13–18

Don't gloat when your enemy falls, and don't let your heart rejoice when he stumbles. Proverbs 24:17

What does it mean to gloat? The dictionary says it means to "gaze in malicious pleasure" at someone else's misfortune. Sounds pretty cold-hearted, doesn't it? It takes a low character to find pleasure in someone else's pain.

But what if the hurting person had it coming? What if he's been a source of pain and grief in your life? What if he deliberately set out to hurt you, but it backfired on him? Isn't it natural to find just a little satisfaction when your enemies are getting what they deserve?

Natural, yes. But God's way, no. The Bible says that it's God business to see that justice is done, not ours. Instead, we're free to respond to those who hurt us by loving them, praying for them, and forgiving them.

If we don't do that—if we choose to gloat over our enemy—it reveals that we, too, have evil in our hearts and that we're no better than the person who injured us. When we're happy to see a person falling under God's discipline (as it says in verse 18 of today's passage), the Lord may release our enemy and turn his discipline on us.

If you find yourself taking pleasure in someone else's pain, recognize that you are sinning. Hurry to seek God's forgiveness, and ask him to help you see your enemy through Christ's loving eyes. When you see someone as God does, you won't feel like gloating.

WHAT DIFFERENT FORMS CAN LOVING YOUR ENEMIES TAKE?

READ UP: NUMBERS 14:11–19 • 2 SAMUEL 18:28–33

BREAKING THE CYCLE

READ AHEAD: PROVERBS 24:28–29

Don't say, "I'll do to him what he did to me; I'll repay the man for what he has done." Proverbs 24:29

There are two ways to live your life: proactively or reactively.

Living proactively involves setting a high standard for your behavior, not letting the sinful influence of others drag you down. Your guide for this way of life is the Bible. That's where you'll learn how God wants you to treat yourself and how he wants you to relate to others.

This doesn't mean you look down on everyone else or that you think of yourself as perfect. But it does mean you consciously follow a pattern of behavior that honors God, rather than living your life in response to what everyone else is doing.

Living reactively means constantly taking your cue from other people. If people gossip about you, you'll take that as permission to gossip about them. If a friend treats you poorly, you'll consider it an invitation to treat your friend poorly in return.

The problem with living reactively is that you lose control over your own life. You spend so much time responding to real or perceived injustices, you have no energy left to live as God wants you to live.

Instead of acting the way everyone else acts, or treating people exactly as they treat you, seek to raise the standard of your behavior. Break the cycle of sin by acting with integrity and setting a good example, regardless of what others are doing.

WHY ARE STANDARDS NOT ALWAYS VERY DIFFERENT BETWEEN CHRISTIANS AND NON-CHRISTIANS?

READ UP: DANIEL 6:3–10 • MATTHEW 5:38–42

GOLDEN APPLES

READ AHEAD: PROVERBS 25:11–15

A word spoken at the right time is like golden apples on a silver tray. Proverbs 25:11

Anyone can dish up compliments, especially if he's trying to get something in return for the praise. That's called *flattery*.

Anyone can criticize under the pretense of "just being honest." That's called *judging*.

But the truth spoken in love at the appropriate time takes wisdom. It's genuine, "like golden apples on a silver tray," and much more valuable.

The difference between these can be very subtle. For instance, your friend might come to you under deep conviction for his sin. You want to spare his feelings, so you try to convince him it's not that big a deal. You're saying nice words, but you're not doing your friend any favors. Yes, he needs your kindness, but if the Holy Spirit is making him uncomfortable with his sin, you shouldn't try to make him comfortable with it.

On the other hand, you might speak the truth but say it with all the wrong motives. When a friend is suffering—even if it's because of her own choices—that's not the time to point out all the shortcomings that got her into her predicament. What she needs more than criticism is kindness. Don't use her vulnerability as a springboard to launch into sharing all her imperfections.

To be sure you use your words properly, always put your listener's best interests first. Be sensitive to what God wants to say through you, and you'll deliver a blessing to someone who really needs one.

WHAT ALL IS INVOLVED IN BEING SOMEONE WHO HAS THE RIGHT WORD AT THE RIGHT TIME?

READ UP: JOHN 11:21–27 • COLOSSIANS 4:5–6

TOMORROW CAN WAIT

READ AHEAD: PROVERBS 27:1–2

Don't boast about tomorrow, for you don't know what a day might bring. Proverbs 27:1

Some people live as if there's no tomorrow, but that's not what this proverb is talking about.

True, only a fool lives without any regard for the future, as though there will be no consequences for his actions. Only a fool lives for the present only, not bothering to put much effort into school, for example, because he thinks his career will just happen automatically.

But while the Bible doesn't advise us to live as if tomorrow will never come, it does caution us against worrying about the future. God has far too much for you to experience of him today for you to waste even a moment worrying about tomorrow.

The Bible also warns us against making our own plans without regard for what God might ask of us. It's a waste of a Christian's time to make extensive plans for your future when you haven't consulted with God first. God is in control of tomorrow, just as he is in control of today.

So the main question to ask yourself is: "What does God want me to do today?" That will keep you busy enough, without having to worry about what might happen tomorrow. If you spend each day in God's will, and if you follow him step by step, your future will unfold as it should.

WHAT DO YOU THINK GOD HAS IN MIND FOR YOU . . . JUST FOR TODAY?

READ UP: MATTHEW 6:25–34 • JAMES 4:13–17

TRUE FRIENDS

READ AHEAD: PROVERBS 27:4–6

The wounds of a friend are trustworthy, but the kisses of an enemy are excessive. Proverbs 27:6

A friend you can trust is a priceless treasure. So consider yourself very wealthy if you have a trustworthy friend, and never take the friendship for granted. This kind of friend is:

• *Honest.* He'll be kind, but he won't dish out flattery in order to hold on to your friendship. In turn, a real friend will listen to you when you speak the truth in love, and will accept constructive criticism, even when it hurts.

• *Reliable.* She'll not stab you in the back or spread gossip about you. An authentic friend puts your interests ahead of her own. She doesn't act out of selfish motives but out of genuine concern for your well-being.

Wouldn't it be great to have a friend like that? Wouldn't it be great to *be* a friend like that?

There are others who only *appear* to be your friend. They spend time with you for what they receive instead of what they give. They tell you what they think you want to hear instead of what you *need* to hear. They have ulterior motives for being your friend, motives you can't trust. These are the kinds of friends to avoid!

In all of your friendships, strive to treat the other person the way you'd like to be treated. Be the best friend you can be, and let God worry about what you'll get in return for your kindness.

WHAT DREW YOU TO THE FRIENDS YOU HAVE NOW?

READ UP: PROVERBS 17:17 • PROVERBS 18:24

LOOK SHARP

READ AHEAD: PROVERBS 27:17–19

Iron sharpens iron, and one man sharpens another. Proverbs 27:17

All the self-help books in the world can't do for you what a true friend can do. Just as the wrong kind of friends can do you immeasurable harm, a good friend can do you incredible good. Two pieces of iron left on the ground to rust are useless. But if those pieces are used to sharpen each other, both become valuable.

The Christian life is a journey that God doesn't expect you to make on your own. He'll bring friends alongside you to help you become the best person you can be.

A good friend sometimes walks ahead of you, showing you how to live by example. Sometimes he walks beside you, helping you when the path is rough. At other times she walks behind you, encouraging you to keep moving in the right direction. If you have a friendship like this, thank God for it, because it's a gift from him.

As you strive to be all that God wants you to be, open yourself up to your friends so they can help you along the way. Seek to be the kind of person who's always sensitive to the concerns of your friends. Search for friends who will be a positive influence on your life. Make the effort to be the kind of friend who helps others reach their potential. Ask yourself if your friends are better off with or without your influence.

If you don't have a friendship that is mutually uplifting, ask God to help you develop one.

WHAT ALL GOES INTO THE SHARPENING PROCESS?

READ UP: LUKE 22:31–32 • HEBREWS 10:24–25

MY COMPLIMENTS

READ AHEAD: PROVERBS 27:21–24

Silver is tested in a crucible, gold in a smelter, and a man, by the praise he receives. Proverbs 27:21

Be careful that you don't draw your conclusions about your character from what others say about you. They only see the part that you present to them. But what others see on the outside and what's really there on the inside can sometimes be two different things!

For example, you could acquire the reputation of being a generous person by making sure others often see you in the act of giving. But in reality, you might only give when someone is watching. You may, in fact, have a selfish character, but you do your taking in private and your giving in public.

We all want to present the best possible picture to the world. But God's opinion of us is far more important than man's is. While your friends may praise you for your self-control, God knows if you're actually prone to angry fits of rage at home when the curtains are closed.

So never be lulled into complacency by the high opinions of others. Remember, God is more interested in your character than in your reputation. Allow him to refine your character and burn away all the impurities until you are truly like Christ.

Your character is (or should be) a highly valuable treasure to you. You may think you have a pretty good handle on what your character is like, but if you listen carefully to what God says about you, what you hear may surprise you!

HOW DO YOU HANDLE A COMPLIMENT?

READ UP: LUKE 6:20–26 • JOHN 2:23–25

CONFESSION

READ AHEAD: PROVERBS 28:9–13

The one who conceals his sins will not prosper, but whoever confesses and renounces them will find mercy. Proverbs 28:13

Unconfessed sin is the most needless form of self-punishment there is. Whenever you hold on to your sin and try to conceal it . . .

• *You'll be plagued by worries.* "Do others know what I've done?" "When will the truth come out?"

• *You'll be weighed down by guilt and shame.* "How could I have been so stupid?" "Can the one I offended ever forgive me?" "Can God ever forgive me?"

• *You'll be dragged down into deception.* "If I tell just one more lie, my secret will still be safe."

The sad thing is, it's so unnecessary. God already knows you've sinned. He doesn't need you to confess it for his benefit. He needs you to confess it for your own good.

Unconfessed sin will always have mastery over you. It will eat away at you like a disease. The last place you may want to be is in the presence of God, but that's the first place you should go.

Let him help you see the damage your sin has done so you won't be tempted to do it again. Let him give you the strength to turn your back on your sin. Let him give you the courage to seek forgiveness from whomever you've sinned against. Let him love you, forgive you, cleanse you, and give you a new start.

WHEN HAS SIN EVER DELIVERED ON ITS PROMISES?

READ UP: DANIEL 9:4–19 • 1 JOHN 1:5–10

STAYING IN SHAPE

READ AHEAD: PROVERBS 28:14–20

Happy is the one who is always reverent, but one who hardens his heart falls into trouble. Proverbs 28:14

Why can some people go through life's dark valleys and never lose their faith in God, while others turn their backs on him at the first sign of hardship? It's the same reason some people can run a marathon, while others can't climb a flight of stairs without stopping to catch their breath.

It all depends on the condition they're in.

The reason some people can trust in God when the big problems come is because they've trusted him all along in the little things. They've conditioned their hearts by spending regular time with God. They've watched him at work all around them, and they've listened for his voice, even when there was no crisis.

Others may have gradually turned away from God, possibly without even realizing it. Perhaps they found it more comfortable to stay in bed than to get up and spend time with God. Then they gradually pulled out of church. Before they knew it, their hearts were no longer sensitive to God's leading. They no longer heard his voice. When a crisis hit, they found themselves alone and in trouble.

Take an honest look at your own heart's condition. Are you still tender toward God, or are you pulling away from him? If you sense cynicism creeping into your life, spend some quality time in God's Word. Pray that he will soften your heart so you can stay with him for the whole race.

WHAT WOULD HAPPEN TO SOMEONE WHO TRIED TO RUN A MARATHON WITHOUT TRAINING FOR IT?

READ UP: 1 CORINTHIANS 9:24–27 • HEBREWS 5:11–14

AFRAID TO MAKE A MOVE

READ AHEAD: PROVERBS 29:23–27

The fear of man is a snare, but the one who trusts in the Lord is protected. Proverbs 29:25

Christians often talk about looking for God's will. We act as if he were playing hide-and-seek with us, trying to make his desires as obscure as possible.

Most often, though, we already know what he wants us to do, yet fear prevents us from doing it! We fear failure. We fear the unknown. We fear what others will think of us.

Fearing other people is a common trap for Christians. We want to obey God, but we don't want to ruffle anyone's feathers in the process. Therefore we don't speak up against something we know is wrong, or we stay in an unhealthy friendship even though God tells us it's wrong for us.

Sometimes when God tells us to do something, the fear of embarrassment stops us from doing it. For example, we know God wants us to be baptized, but we wouldn't be caught dead in front of our congregation with a wet head!

Sometimes, it can get even closer to home than that. Perhaps your parents disapprove of your Christianity, so in an attempt to please them, you dishonor God. In your quest to please everyone around you, you can end up doing the very opposite of what you know God wants.

It's not always possible to fear God and man at the same time. But God's love for you far surpasses anything you might fear from man.

HOW BIG DO YOU THINK YOUR CURRENT FEARS WILL APPEAR TEN YEARS FROM NOW?

READ UP: PSALM 56:3–9 • LUKE 12:4–7

WHAT'S YOUR OVERALL TAKE ON PROVERBS?

THE LORD'S PRAYER

PRAYER IS ABSOLUTELY ONE OF THE MOST IMPORTANT THINGS A CHRISTIAN WILL EVER DO. When we pray, we talk directly with the God of the universe. He speaks to us, and we tell him our concerns. It's not difficult to pray, yet not many Christians claim to pray as much as they should.

It's interesting to note, though, that during all the time the disciples spent with Jesus . . .

• *They never asked him to teach them how to preach*, even though he sent them out to preach throughout the countryside.

• *They never asked him for instructions on how to teach*, even though this would later become an important part of their duties as apostles.

• *They never asked to be shown how to perform miracles or cast out demons*, even though the Scripture reveals they were empowered to do this.

Their one request for instruction was: "Lord, teach us to pray" (Luke 11:1). Something about the way Jesus prayed compelled the disciples to want to be like him. Truly, some of the most profound times in Jesus' life happened right after he prayed.

When Jesus taught his disciples the Lord's Prayer, he wasn't giving them a prayer to memorize and recite every time they prayed. He was simply giving them a model for their own prayers.

As you study the model prayer that Jesus gave—as you read it and re-read it for eight straight days—compare it with the prayers you offer to God. What can you learn from the way Jesus prayed that can help you to be more effective in your own praying?

ALL TOGETHER NOW

READ AHEAD: MATTHEW 6:9–13

Therefore, you should pray like this: Our Father in heaven . . .
Matthew 6:9

God designed the family to be a source of love and encouragement. If you have a family who loves you and is in your corner, it's much easier for you to take on life with confidence.

But what if your family is constantly critical, angry, or even abusive? Then you must remember that you have another family—your Christian family—who longs to love and support you.

The Lord's Prayer opens with the familiar word "our," a plural pronoun that reminds us we are not alone. We're part of a family, complete with a loving, heavenly Father, as well as brothers and sisters at home and around the world. Through them we can find the strength and encouragement we need to face life's ups and downs.

But this is a spiritual blessing that truly goes both ways. Just as God has called others to minister to us, he has also called us to love and serve our Christian family members.

So we ought never to pray with only ourselves in mind. If we pray with selfish motives, without concern for our fellow believers, the Bible says our prayers are of the devil (James 3:14–15). If we pray while we are angry and unforgiving toward other Christians, God will frown on our prayers (Matthew 5:22–24).

Every time we pray, God wants us to remember that we are part of a family who is precious to him.

WHY DID GOD CHOOSE THE PICTURE OF A FAMILY TO DESCRIBE HIS PEOPLE?

READ UP: 1 CORINTHIANS 12:12–18 • GALATIANS 3:27–28

OUR FATHER

READ AHEAD: MATTHEW 6:9-13

Our Father . . . Matthew 6:9

When you hear the term "father," what comes to your mind? Without realizing it, you probably equate God's character with the way you view your earthly father. Perhaps your father is nurturing, affectionate, and reliable. If so, you'll probably see God that way, too.

But sadly, some fathers are harsh and critical, even cruel. If your father neglects you or doesn't express love toward you, you may tend to think God is uncaring. When you go through hard times, you may assume it's futile to seek comfort from him. When you have a need, you might conclude, "There's no point in asking God. He won't provide for me."

But rather than trying to fit God into your image of what a father is like, realize that even fathers with the best of intentions make mistakes and have weak moments. No father loves his children the way God does. He's never too busy or preoccupied or self-centered to care about you. And because his love is unconditional, you'll always find forgiveness when you seek it from him, no matter how many times you blow it by sinning.

Spend some time getting to know your Father in heaven. Allow him to love you as only he can. Receive his discipline as proof that, while he will not be lenient with you, he will never give up on you. He wants so much for you to experience the peace and joy that only he can give.

WHAT ARE SOME THINGS YOUR HEAVENLY FATHER IS NOT?

READ UP: PSALM 27:7-10 • ISAIAH 49:14-16

ABOVE, NOT BEYOND

READ AHEAD: MATTHEW 6:9–13

Our Father in heaven . . . Matthew 6:9

Where is God when you pray? What did Jesus mean when he said his Father was "in heaven"?

He didn't mean God is up there somewhere where you can't reach him. He was reminding his followers that God is not limited like we are, and that we should approach him much differently than we approach others.

Other people—even our close friends and family—are restricted by what they can do (or will do) for us. When we communicate with them, we're dealing with people who are neither perfect nor all-powerful. When we speak to God, however, we're talking with one who is eternal, who rules the universe, who is able to arrange our lives so precisely that we always remain in the center of his will and protection.

So think and meditate on God's greatness as you pray:

- Remember that nothing is impossible for him.
- He is holy and righteous, so he will not overlook your sin.
- But he is merciful and will forgive you when you ask.
- He loves you more deeply than you can ever imagine.
- And he will answer your prayers in ways that are best for you.

Don't be in a hurry to rush in and out of God's presence. Let the knowledge that you are talking to Almighty God dramatically affect the way you pray.

WHAT WAS GOD'S PURPOSE IN GIVING US PRAYER?

READ UP: ROMANS 11:33–36 • REVELATION 4:9–11

PRAISE HIS NAME

READ AHEAD: MATTHEW 6:9–13

Your name be honored as holy. Matthew 6:9

Names aren't what they used to be. In biblical times, parents gave their children names that they hoped would reflect the child's character. They believed that knowing a person's name gave some insight into his or her personality.

When Jacob was born, for example, he was grasping his twin brother, Esau, by the heel (Genesis 25:26). So his parents named him Jacob, meaning "he grasps the heel," or "deceiver." True to his name, Jacob grew up to take advantage of his brother at every opportunity.

Sometimes people even had their names changed after they became adults. When Andrew brought his brother, Simon, to meet Jesus, the Bible records, "When Jesus saw him, He said, 'You are Simon, son of John. You will be called Cephas [or Peter],' which means 'Rock'" (John 1:42).

With this cultural background in mind, we can see the importance in Jesus' words regarding God's name. Because God is perfectly holy, we acknowledge the sacredness of his character every time we call on his name. The very name "Lord" is a reminder that the one we address is divine and worthy of our deepest reverence.

Jesus wants us to know that when we pray, we are actually speaking to Almighty God. If we realize this at the front end of our prayer, we'll be less inclined to ask him for anything that would dishonor his holy name.

WHAT ARE SOME OTHER NAMES OR CHARACTER TRAITS ASCRIBED TO GOD IN THE BIBLE?

READ UP: PSALM 96:1–13 • ISAIAH 6:1–3

WANTING GOD'S WILL

READ AHEAD: MATTHEW 6:9–13

Your kingdom come. Your will be done on earth as it is in heaven.
Matthew 6:10

No arguments are ever waged in heaven over obeying God's will. The angels don't spend weeks mulling over whether or not they'll do what God is telling them. They simply obey—immediately, completely, and cheerfully.

If only we would do the same! Some of us spend a lot of time seeking God's will. But if we'd spend as much time doing what we already know God wants us to do, the rest would take care of itself.

"Your kingdom come" is really a request for God to bring about his rule over every person on earth. It means turning our gaze away from ourselves, choosing to look outward to the work God is doing around us.

Of course, we can't pray earnestly for God to have his way over every other person's life if God is not the Lord of our own lives. This prayer must begin with us. Only when God is the ruler over our lives can we sincerely pray for him to have complete rule over our families, neighbors, classmates, and friends.

So when we pray like this, we must be prepared to be part of God's answer. If God is to rule in our friend's life, God may want to use us to make her aware of his love. Praying for God's kingdom to come is not enough. We must be ready to get up on our feet and go out as Christ's messenger to those who have not yet claimed him as their Lord.

WHAT ARE SOME THINGS YOU ALREADY KNOW GOD WANTS YOU TO DO?

READ UP: JOHN 18:36–37 • COLOSSIANS 1:9–14

DAILY BREAD

READ AHEAD: MATTHEW 6:9–13

Give us today our daily bread. Matthew 6:11

We know God can do big things when we ask, but we assume some requests are beneath him—too small to bother the Lord of the universe with. Not so. Jesus used the example of bread to teach us this truth.

Bread was the most common element of a Jewish meal. Nothing could have been considered more ordinary. They didn't always eat rich, elaborate feasts, but they had bread every day.

To the disciples, then, daily bread represented the unspectacular. They'd seen Jesus heal disease, calm storms, and walk on water. They knew God could deliver the big-ticket items. But Jesus was telling them not to leave God out of the seemingly ordinary parts of life.

Praying every day for God to meet our needs doesn't annoy him. On the contrary, it pleases him. Asking for our daily bread is also a regular reminder to ourselves that we rely on God for everything—not just the big things, but the everyday needs of life.

Don't ever worry that God will consider your needs too small for him. He loves you. He wants to take care of you whether you need a miracle or a piece of bread. Remember that everything in life comes from God. Don't forget to thank him today for meeting even your most basic needs.

WHAT ARE SOME OF THE MOST MUNDANE THINGS YOU COULD THINK OF TO THANK GOD FOR?

READ UP: DEUTERONOMY 8:12–18 • 1 TIMOTHY 6:6–10

LET IT GO

READ AHEAD: MATTHEW 6:9–13

Forgive us our debts, as we also have forgiven our debtors.
Matthew 6:12

What's your reaction when someone hurts you or mistreats you? Do you immediately start planning your revenge? That's the world's way of dealing with conflict.

But Jesus shows us a better way—forgiveness. He calls on us to forgive those who offend us, just as God has forgiven us and continues to forgive our sins against him.

The Bible says that we will be treated the same way we treat others (Luke 6:37–38). That can be either a welcome promise or a worrisome thought! If we're generous toward others, we know we will experience God's generosity. But if we refuse to forgive those who wrong us, God will not forgive our sins. Why would he do this?

• *Because he loves us.* He refuses to let us live with sinful attitudes that will eventually destroy us.

• *Because he is making something of us.* He wants to develop a character in us to match his own.

• *Because he is perfectly just.* He won't treat us one way and yet allow us to treat others a different way.

The Lord's Prayer holds the reminder that if we hope to receive forgiveness and grace, we must be willing to extend mercy to those who offend us. When you let go of a grudge, you will experience the joy and freedom that comes with forgiveness.

WHAT ARE THE COSTS OF FORGIVING . . . AND OF NOT FORGIVING?

READ UP: ACTS 7:54–60 • 2 CORINTHIANS 2:5–11

SAFE AND SECURE

READ AHEAD: MATTHEW 6:9–13

Do not bring us into temptation, but deliver us from the evil one.
Matthew 6:13

A time will come—or may have come already—when you find yourself facing intense temptation. You may be asked to compromise in the area of sex, lying, or stealing. Others may pressure you to get into alcohol, drugs, or gambling. Even when you don't go out deliberately looking for it, the powerful voice of temptation can still call to you, and you can quickly come to the edge of giving in.

Sin is a serious thing. Never forget that. Its goal is our destruction. But too often we like to get as close to temptation as we can. We think we'll be strong enough to pull back at the last minute. Then to our dismay, we discover that temptation is not as easily resisted as we thought. Sin is a much more powerful foe than we realize.

Don't walk blindly through life, spiritually weak and unprepared for the temptations you'll meet. Every day when you pray . . .

• Ask God to protect you from evil.

• Ask him to keep you from situations that can overpower you.

• Ask him to guide you into his will, away from anything that could sidetrack you or destroy you.

Don't wait until you're hopelessly entangled in sin to ask God to help you. Ask him to deliver you from evil now, while there's still time to avoid disaster.

IN WHAT WAY HAVE YOU EVER EXPERIENCED GOD'S HAND PROTECTING YOU FROM SIN?

READ UP: NEHEMIAH 6:1–14 • PSALM 27:1–3

ANYTHING UNEXPECTED YOU SAW IN THE LORD'S PRAYER?

SAY IT AGAIN, SAM

SAMUEL WAS ONE OF THE SPIRITUAL GIANTS OF THE OLD TESTAMENT, WHOSE LIFE STORY IS TOLD IN THE FIRST OF TWO BOOKS THAT BEAR HIS NAME.

His entire life was dedicated to serving God. Even his birth was a result of the prayers of his mother, Hannah, who had never been able to have children until God blessed her with Samuel, her baby boy.

As a result, Samuel knew beyond the shadow of a doubt—from a very young age—that God had a purpose for his life. In accordance with his mother's prayers, he even went to live full-time in the temple as a youth, learning at the feet of godly leaders and discovering how to hear God speaking to him. As a result, he had many years—a whole lifetime— to walk intimately with God.

He was also a person of integrity, living so blamelessly that (according to 1 Samuel 12:4) no one could find fault with him. His walk with God was so powerful, even kings were afraid of him.

But the really encouraging thing about Samuel is that he was no different from us. He had no unusual intelligence or ability to hear from God. He simply started walking with God when he was a young person and—gradually, over time—he became one of the greatest saints of the Bible.

As we look at a few scenes from his life over the next four days, watch carefully to see how Samuel learned to walk with God. By following his example, there's no reason why you, too, can't have a walk with God that is equally strong, close, and powerful.

GOD'S FROM THE START

READ AHEAD: 1 SAMUEL 1:1–18

I will give him to the Lord all the days of his life.
1 Samuel 1:11

Samuel grew up knowing he was born for a unique purpose.

His birth itself had been an answer to his mother's impassioned prayers. She prayed that if God would give her a child, she would dedicate him to God. It wasn't as though Samuel had no choice in how he lived, but he wisely chose to follow the path that God set out for him. He never had to worry about an identity crisis. He lived his entire life secure in the knowledge that God had created him for a purpose.

You, too, can be sure that your life has great meaning. God created you intentionally—not accidentally—and he has a purpose for you. You're probably unaware, in fact, of just how many prayers God has heard with your name attached to them. Long before you were born, godly ancestors may have been praying that their children and grandchildren would trust and follow God. Even if your parents aren't Christians, you may have no idea how many times others have prayed specifically for you.

So don't ever think your life is insignificant. God has had his hand on you from the very beginning. You matter a great deal to him, and he still has much that he wants to do through your life.

Take time today to celebrate your uniqueness. Thank him for the faithful people who have prayed for you over the years, and praise him for answering those prayers.

WHAT KINDS OF BIG PRAYERS DO YOU REGULARLY PRAY FOR YOURSELF AND FOR OTHERS YOU LOVE?

READ UP: PSALM 139:13–16 • JEREMIAH 1:4–9

RECOGNIZING GOD'S VOICE

READ AHEAD: 1 SAMUEL 3:1–10

Samuel responded, "Speak, for Your servant is listening."
1 Samuel 3:10

Perhaps you know a man or woman who, like Samuel, seems to have an inside track with God. Do you wish you knew the Lord like that?

You know what, though? Even the most godly Christians you know started out just like everyone else—as strangers to God, not accustomed to the way he works, spiritually disoriented and learning on the go.

Samuel was no exception. When God first called out to him, he didn't even recognize who was speaking! He assumed it was Eli, the priest. That's because Samuel, too, had to learn how to recognize God's voice and understand what God was saying to him. But after years of spending time with God, he was able to recognize his voice instantly.

There's no other way to learn how to identify God's voice than to spend time talking with him. Samuel took advantage of every opportunity he had to get to know God. As a result, God did great things through Samuel's life.

The exciting thing is, you have the same opportunity as the greatest spiritual giants you know. God will speak to you just as he speaks to them. You may not always recognize God's voice now, but continue spending time with him. The day will come when you won't have to wonder if it's God speaking. You'll know who it is.

WHAT HAVE YOU LEARNED SO FAR ABOUT THE WAY GOD COMMUNICATES WITH YOU?

READ UP: JOHN 16:12–14 • ACTS 11:4–17

PRAY ANYWAY

READ AHEAD: 1 SAMUEL 12:19–25

As for me, I vow that I will not sin against the Lord by ceasing to pray for you. 1 Samuel 12:23

God appointed Samuel as Israel's spiritual guide because the Lord didn't want his people to have a secular king like other nations had. He wanted them to be different and distinct, to trust in God and listen to his spokesmen—people like Samuel.

But the Israelites had other ideas. They whined. They pleaded. They begged for a king. Samuel warned them that they were only asking for trouble, but they persisted in their demands. So finally, God gave them what they wanted.

Poor Samuel, then, had to lead the national dedication ceremony for the person Israel had rejected him for.

But once the people got what they wanted, they realized their mistake. They turned back to Samuel and begged him to continue ministering to them. If there was ever a time for an "I-told-you-so," this was it! Fortunately for Israel, however, Samuel was more mature than that. He knew if he gave up on God's people, they would be in even worse trouble, so he swallowed his pride and stuck with them.

Your friends will not always thank you for warning them when they're heading into dangerous territory. They may reject your advice. They may even reject *you*. Even though it hurts, resist the temptation to abandon them to their own foolishness. Continue to pray for them, and be ready to forgive them when they realize their mistake. Wouldn't you want them to do the same for you?

HOW DID YOU HANDLE YOUR LAST "I-TOLD-YOU-SO" MOMENT?

READ UP: ACTS 3:13–19 • JAMES 5:19–20

OH YEAH?

READ AHEAD: 1 SAMUEL 15:1–14

Samuel replied, "Then what is this sound of sheep and cattle I hear?" 1 Samuel 15:14

God's instructions to Saul had been clear: take no possessions from the enemy, but destroy everyone and everything as an act of judgment on them. Still, Saul couldn't resist pilfering some of the enemy's best animals. ("What a shame to waste perfectly good livestock?") He also spared the wicked king's life. ("Why not give the guy a break?")

Then he made things worse by lying to Samuel, boasting in front of the people about how he had followed God's instructions. Samuel was no fool. He knew the truth. But Saul was still the king. You don't advance your career by embarrassing the king in front of his subjects.

Sometimes it's a lot less trouble to look the other way than it is to confront sin. It's tempting to rationalize that your friends are just having some fun, that it's really none of your business. You don't want to look like a prude. Besides, you know you're not perfect yourself.

Yet God expects you to do as Samuel did—to see sin for what it is. It's not like he was going around looking to see how many faults he could find in others. On the other hand, he wasn't about to stand there and let Saul insult God's name through his blatant disobedience—especially when Saul was calling his sin *obedience!*

When you're in a situation where others are trying to disguise their sin, pray for the courage to resist compromising with the truth.

WHEN HAVE YOU LAST FELT THE NEED TO CONFRONT SOMEONE OVER A PARTICULAR SIN?

READ UP: MATTHEW 18:15–17 • GALATIANS 6:1–2

128

WHAT DO YOU LIKE ABOUT SAMUEL'S STRENGTHS?

REAL LIFE CHRISTIANITY

TO WALK IN LOVE WITH SAINTS ABOVE,
O! THAT WILL BE PURE GLORY!
TO WALK BELOW WITH SAINTS WE KNOW,
NOW THAT'S ANOTHER STORY!

The person who wrote this poem was an astute observer of God's people. The Christian life is always easier to study than it is to practice!

If all we ever had to do, for example, was affirm that it's good to love our enemies, we'd all be spiritual giants. But when God asks us to love one of our *real* enemies, that's when our high-sounding theories fly out the window!

Learning to live in harmony with other believers is an essential part of being a Christian. God does not call us to be lone-ranger Christians. He wants us to work together. He commands us to love one another and to forgive our fellow believers when they sin against us. He instructs us to love even those who seem unlovable.

That's God's intention for the church—a place where Christians can work together, meet each other's needs, and carry each other's burdens. We pray together and study the Bible together. We learn together how to be everything God has called us to be. The church isn't perfect, because its members aren't perfect. But the church is definitely God's way for his people to operate.

As you read the following six devotions, ask yourself if you're serving God in your church the way the Bible says you should.

THE BLAME GAME

READ AHEAD: GENESIS 3:8–13

The man replied, "The woman You gave to be with me—she gave me some fruit from the tree, and I ate." Genesis 3:12

This habit of looking for a scapegoat is nothing new. After Adam and Eve ate from the forbidden tree, the first thing they did was to look around for someone to blame. It was slim pickings, though, since they comprised the entire population of the Garden of Eden. Yet they each managed to find someone:

Adam: "The woman you gave to be with me—she . . ."

Eve: "It was the serpent. He deceived me."

God didn't fall for either of their excuses, of course. But this hasn't stopped generations of sinners from trying the same trick:

- "I didn't know it was a sin."
- "My friends tricked me."
- "I don't have a strong support network in my church."
- "Everyone makes mistakes."
- (And of course, the old classic) "Satan was oppressing me!"

Why waste your breath? When God confronts you with your sin, you can offer him a thousand reasons for why you did it, but only one will hold up: "Forgive me, Lord. I was wrong." It's incredibly freeing when you go ahead and admit your fault and seek forgiveness. Think of how different this world would be if every one of us accepted responsibility for our own behavior!

BE HONEST. IN WHAT WAYS DO YOU TRY SUGARCOATING YOUR SINS?

READ UP: 1 KINGS 8:33–36 • LUKE 22:55–62

SPEAK UP

READ AHEAD: ACTS 2:1–8

How is it that we hear, each of us, in our own native language?
Acts 2:8

Not long after Jesus' resurrection and ascension, God sent his Holy Spirit to the believers in Jerusalem. When they received the Spirit, they began to speak in languages they had never spoken before.

At the time, there were many foreigners in Jerusalem whose native language was not Hebrew. When these visitors heard a commotion, they gathered around to see what was going on. To their astonishment, each of them heard the gospel presented in his or her native tongue. They were flabbergasted! Over a dozen countries were represented in the crowd, yet every person heard the good news that day, even though the ones doing the speaking didn't know what they were saying.

When God wants you to share his message, don't be intimidated by the circumstances. You may feel inadequate to share Christ's love because you don't know what to say. If you're a new Christian, you may think you don't know the Bible well enough. Don't let that stop you. God gave you his Holy Spirit to help you spread his good news effectively (Acts 1:8).

And don't assume God will only use you to reach out to people who are just like you. His Spirit will guide you as you share his love, even with those who are very different from you. The important thing is that you're open to talk about your faith as the Holy Spirit prompts you.

WHY DO WE TEND TO UNDERESTIMATE WHAT GOD CAN DO THROUGH US?

READ UP: EXODUS 4:10–15 • ACTS 1:6–8

BACK TO BASICS

READ AHEAD: ACTS 2:41–43

They devoted themselves to the apostles' teaching, to fellowship, to the breaking of bread, and to prayers. Acts 2:42

There are all sorts of churches. Each has a different personality and expresses itself in a variety of ways. But it makes no difference what the building looks like or whether the pastor wears a black robe or blue jeans. The important thing is that the church is biblical.

Churches based on the Bible have at least four things in common:

• *Learning.* The apostles were set aside as teachers in the early church because they had walked with Jesus and because he had commanded them to make disciples. God still calls out and equips people to teach others about Christ.

• *Fellowship.* God didn't design the Christian life to be a lone, solitary venture. He wants us to encourage one another, enjoy one another, and build wholesome relationships with other Christians.

• *Worship.* The breaking of bread probably referred to the Lord's Supper. The early church met regularly for the purpose of worshiping and remembering Christ's death and resurrection. In other words, they gathered to remind themselves why they existed.

• *Prayer.* This was the lifeline of the first church, as it is for us today. If your church is not a praying church, you will not know what Christ wants you to do. There is too much at stake for us to think we can survive without prayer.

Don't get distracted by the differences between your church and somebody else's. The Bible tells us what's really important.

HOW WOULD YOU DESCRIBE A MODEL CHURCH?

READ UP: ACTS 17:10–12 • COLOSSIANS 1:3–8

BIG US, LITTLE ME

READ AHEAD: ACTS 2:44–45

Now all the believers were together and had everything in common.
Acts 2:44

Early Christians loved to be together. The experience of Christianity was so new and exciting to them, they wanted to celebrate their faith with other believers. To first-century Christians, church wasn't a once-a-week thing. It was an everyday occurrence.

The first church was characterized by a "we" mentality. Those who had something to give shared it willingly. They wouldn't think of enjoying a full pantry while their fellow believers went hungry. If someone needed shelter, others opened their homes. If someone needed money, others sold stuff to get it. They demonstrated church the way Jesus meant it to be—vibrant, alive, supportive, loving, giving, sharing, fun.

Would you like to help your church become more like this one? Here are a few suggestions to get you started:

- Invite people from church into your home.
- Share something you have with someone who needs it.
- Linger after each service and meet someone you don't know.
- Go to a church function in addition to Sunday morning.
- Offer to serve in a specific ministry.

As you open yourself up to your church, an amazing thing will happen. You'll see your church more as a family and less as an institution. You'll discover the joy God intends for his people to experience.

WHAT DO YOU NEED FROM YOUR CHURCH? WHAT DO THEY NEED FROM YOU?

READ UP: 1 THESSALONIANS 3:6–13 • PHILEMON 4–7

THIS IS FUN!

READ AHEAD: ACTS 2:46–47

Every day they devoted themselves to meeting together in the temple complex, and broke bread from house to house. Acts 2:46

Some Christians feel embarrassed about their faith. They live the Christian life as if it were a burden to carry. They think they have to coerce others to accept Christ. What a tragic misconception! That's not what Christianity is about at all!

Loving God is not a burden. It's a joy! Following Christ isn't something to be hidden. It's an incredible adventure to be shared!

Two thousand years ago, the world was desperate for what the early church had. It was a time of war and unrest, yet the Christians had peace. Poverty was widespread, yet the early church shared generously. First-century believers were noted for the way they loved one another. They were conspicuous because of their joy. They loved to be together. Their relationships went past the superficial. They were more like family than just friends.

So guess what? The Bible says they found "favor with all the people" (verse 47). People liked them because they were different—different in all the good kinds of ways.

As a Christian, you never have to be embarrassed about what you believe. People all around you are searching for something to fill the emptiness within them. They're looking for exactly what you have! So concentrate on living the Christian life with enthusiasm, and be ready to tell others how they can find the same joy they see in you.

WHAT IS IT ABOUT CHRISTIANS THAT EITHER TURNS PEOPLE OFF OR WHETS THEIR APPETITE?

READ UP: ACTS 20:32–38 • 1 THESSALONIANS 2:17–20

DIVINE APPOINTMENTS

READ AHEAD: ACTS 8:26–39

The Spirit told Philip, "Go and join that chariot!" Acts 8:29

Philip was enjoying tremendous success while preaching in Samaria. Many people were turning their lives over to Christ. So Philip could have reasonably concluded that God wanted him to continue preaching there until as many people as possible had become Christians.

Instead, God sent word to Philip to leave what he was doing and to go out into the desert (verse 26). Had the angel gotten his wires crossed? *The desert?* Philip might have thought. *When I'm doing so much good right here? Who am I supposed to preach to out in the desert?*

Yet as strange as God's instructions may have seemed, Philip trusted him and did as he was told.

While Philip was traveling down a desert road, he met an influential Ethiopian in a caravan. The man was reading the Old Testament, but he couldn't understand it. Well, people don't search for answers in the Bible unless God is working in their lives, So immediately, Philip realized what God wanted him to do—help the man become a Christian. Philip simply recognized God's activity and joined in on it.

You never know when God has plans for you to share Christ with someone—perhaps on the school bus or standing in line somewhere. But if you're sensitive to God's leading—even when it doesn't seem all that reasonable—you'll discover the joy of getting involved in God's activity. By keeping a divine appointment, you can have a part in spreading the gospel far beyond yourself!

THINK ABOUT THE SNOWBALL EFFECT YOU CAN SET INTO MOTION WITH ONE WORD OF WITNESS.

READ UP: ACTS 13:46–48 • 1 CORINTHIANS 9:19–23

WHAT'S SO GOOD, AND WHAT'S SO HARD, ABOUT BEING A CHRISTIAN?

FILLING UP ON PHILIPPIANS

When Paul wrote to the Philippians, he was writing to friends. The first person in Europe that Paul helped to know Christ was Lydia, a woman from the city of Philippi (pronounced, *FILL-ih-pie*). Lydia and her family became the nucleus of the first church in Greece.

Also, the local jailer—the one who almost committed suicide after a miraculous earthquake freed Paul from his jail cell—was a part of this church. Paul had introduced him and his family to the joys of knowing Christ. Now they were serving the Lord in the Philippian church.

Another young woman in the church had been demon possessed, but she met Christ when Paul cast out the demon and set her free from her bondage. Needless to say, the people in the Philippian church dearly loved Paul!

So when Paul wrote to his friends in Philippi, he wasn't speaking to strangers. Neither was he trying to come down hard on them, fussing about the immorality and immaturity he dealt with in some of the other churches. Instead, he was giving loving counsel to his friends so they could experience all the wonders of God's love and presence.

Over the next ten days—as we close this book of *TruthQuest* experiences—you'll see the loving guidance Paul gave to his friends in this brand-new church. His advice to them still holds true. So if you want to experience the love and joy Christ has for you, pay close attention to Paul's words in the following devotions—the last ones in this book.

PAUL'S PERSPECTIVE

READ AHEAD: PHILIPPIANS 1:12–20

What does it matter? Just that in every way, whether out of false motives or true, Christ is proclaimed. Philippians 1:18

You'd think Paul would have been discouraged, being chained up in prison for preaching the gospel. You'd think he would've questioned God's wisdom for sidelining one of his best players. After all, who had worked harder to spread the gospel than Paul? Why not send one of the weaker players to the bench and leave Paul on the field?

But he didn't question God's game plan. Instead, he just concentrated on staying faithful—wherever he was—and trusted that God knew what he was doing.

With that kind of attitude, Paul could see that his detainment was actually *helping* spread the gospel: Palace guards were hearing about Christ's love for the first time. Paul's friends were being inspired by his example. Even his enemies were preaching about Christ in an attempt to stir up anger against him. Paul's conclusion? "If Christ is lifted up because of my suffering, then it's all worth it."

When you experience loneliness, criticism, or rejection, don't conclude that God has abandoned you. Trust him to use you in the midst of your situation. Perhaps your critics will be moved by your forgiving attitude, and they'll seek Christ themselves. Your experience might help you learn to be more compassionate toward others who are suffering. Maybe your courage will inspire your friends to take a stand for their faith.

The important thing is to keep your perspective. God is in control, so you have every reason to rejoice!

WHAT'S THE FIRST THOUGHT THAT POPS INTO YOUR HEAD AT THE SIGN OF A BAD DAY?

READ UP: PSALM 119:67–72 • REVELATION 2:8–10

OTHERS FIRST

READ AHEAD: PHILIPPIANS 2:1–4

Do nothing out of rivalry or conceit, but in humility consider others as more important than yourselves. Philippians 2:3

What's the difference between having a healthy self-esteem and being conceited?

If you have a healthy self-esteem, you'll be humble. You'll know that you're who you are because God loves you. You'll understand that God has blessed you because of *his* goodness, not yours. Because you aren't preoccupied with your own importance, you won't mind when others get the attention.

You'll ask others about themselves instead of monopolizing conversations with information about yourself. You'll be comfortable serving others rather than always insisting on what you have coming to you. You'll have a quiet confidence that allows you to build others up instead of tearing them down to make yourself look better.

Conceit, on the other hand, means thinking more of yourself than you should. Whereas humility puts others first, pride stems from your own self-centeredness. It's the tendency to put yourself before others and to focus on your own importance. Pride (oddly enough) can actually grow out of a *low* self-esteem. If you don't like yourself, you might feel the need to brag about your accomplishments just to prove to others (and yourself) that you're worth something. Or you might fake humility in an attempt to get others to build you up.

Ask God to remove your pride and give you true humility, which is not an indication of weakness but a sure sign of healthy self-esteem.

WHAT GIVES HUMILITY ITS WIMPY, MOUSY REPUTATION?

READ UP: PROVERBS 16:18–19 • LUKE 14:7–14

NOTICEABLE CHANGES

READ AHEAD: PHILIPPIANS 2:12–15

Work out your own salvation with fear and trembling.
Philippians 2:12

Everyone comes to the point of salvation from a different experience. Some who accept Christ have been abused, and they've carried bitterness in their hearts for years. But through Christ's example, they learn how to forgive and are no longer slaves of their past.

Others have lived a life of deception. Gossiping and lying are second nature to them. But through Christ, they learn to be honest with themselves and with others.

That's what Paul meant when he said to "work out your salvation." He was saying that new, transformed behavior would come about as a result of being a follower of Christ.

• *Perhaps you've never known a father's love.* Your heavenly Father longs for you to experience his indescribable, unconditional love—to grow in your ability to trust.

• *You may be filled with anger.* Christ can take it away and give you peace in your heart.

• *Are you ashamed of the way you lived before you knew Christ?* He invites you to enjoy the new life his forgiveness has made possible, and to experience the freedom of obedience.

When you accepted Christ, your new life was just beginning. And now—for the rest of your life—God wants to help you live to the fullest. So whatever has prevented you from living the way God desires, let him work in you until your life is completely transformed.

WHAT AREAS IN YOUR LIFE NEED TO BE RENEWED, REWORKED, TRANSFORMED?

READ UP: 2 CORINTHIANS 5:16–17 • 1 JOHN 3:1–3

CHRIST IN CONTRAST

READ AHEAD: PHILIPPIANS 3:3–10

I also consider everything to be a loss in view of the surpassing value of knowing Christ Jesus my Lord. Philippians 3:8

What matters to you more than anything else?

• Your family? Your friends?

• Your reputation? Your health?

• Your grades? Your achievements?

These are all good things. They *should* matter to you. But there's one thing that should come before any of these—knowing Christ.

Before Paul was a Christian, he placed high importance on who he was and where he came from. He took great pride in his pure Jewish heritage, his excellent education, and his flawless behavior. His reputation in the community was everything to him.

Then he met Christ, and everything that used to be on the top of his priority list fell to the bottom. Once he experienced Christ, nothing else could come close! From the moment of his conversion, Paul sent everything else but Christ to the back of the line. As far as Paul was concerned—compared to the value of knowing Christ—everything in his life was as worthless as garbage.

Is knowing Christ that important to you? No one is asking you to stop loving your family, to hate your friends, or to harm your body. But knowing Christ more intimately should be the first item on your priority list. When you choose to place him first in your life, you'll see everything else in its proper perspective.

WHAT DOES THIS KIND OF ATTITUDE MEAN IN PRACTICAL TERMS, IN DAY-TO-DAY LIFE?

READ UP: 1 TIMOTHY 1:12–17 • 2 TIMOTHY 2:8–13

IT'S ALL GOOD

READ AHEAD: PHILIPPIANS 4:1–4

Rejoice in the Lord always. I will say it again: Rejoice!
Philippians 4:4

Have you ever heard the words to the great old hymn "Count Your Blessings"?

When upon life's billows you are tempest tossed,

When you are discouraged, thinking all is lost,

Count your many blessings, name them one by one,

And it will surprise you what the Lord hath done.

There's wisdom for all of us in that old song. Sometimes when we focus on our problems, we lose sight of the good things in our lives. It's as though we're under a gigantic cloud that blocks out the sun. We get irritable and depressed and, worst of all, we lose all perspective. That's when it's time to review all the reasons God has given us for rejoicing.

If you're under the cloud today, try not to grumble and complain. Count your blessings instead. Here's a list to get you started:

- God loves you.
- Jesus died for your sins.
- You'll spend eternity in heaven with Christ.
- You're part of God's family, with brothers and sisters who love you.
- God has promised never to abandon you.

Keep going—thinking of more things—and the cloud will keep lifting.

WHAT ARE SOME UNIQUE, SPECIFIC WAYS GOD HAS BLESSED YOUR LIFE?

READ UP: 1 CHRONICLES 16:8–10 • PSALM 92:1–15

145

WHY WORRY?

READ AHEAD: PHILIPPIANS 4:6–7

Don't worry about anything, but in everything . . . let your requests be made known to God. Philippians 4:6

Anxiety is a thief. It robs our joy, our peace of mind, and even our health. So why do we worry? Because there are so many things to worry about! We all have our own varieties: we worry about getting sick or getting caught, about dying (or about living), about what *has* happened, what *will* happen, what *might* happen, what *isn't* happening . . . or that nothing will *ever* happen!

We might as well face it—there will always be stuff to worry about. So rather than wishing for a problem-free life, we should take Paul's advice: instead of worrying and fretting about everything, we should take our concerns to God.

Paul made a promise attached to this: if you pray about your problems instead of worrying about them, God will give you peace.

Paul couldn't even describe the peace God gives, because it's beyond human description. But he did say God's peace would set up guard duty around your heart and your mind, so that no troublesome worry could disturb them. You'll be free to experience joy because you no longer carry the burden of worrying. When God's peace guards you, you don't have anything left to brood about.

God's peace frees you to live as God wants you to. You'll experience supernatural calmness, no matter what your circumstances. Why not pull out your favorite worry today and turn it over to God?

WHAT ARE THE UNDERLYING ROOTS OF WORRY? WHAT WEAKNESSES DOES IT EXPOSE IN US?

READ UP: ISAIAH 50:7–10 • 2 CORINTHIANS 1:8–10

WHAT'S ON YOUR MIND?

READ AHEAD: PHILIPPIANS 4:8–9

Whatever is true, whatever is honorable, whatever is just, whatever is pure, whatever is lovely, whatever is commendable . . . dwell on these things. Philippians 4:8

Paul seems a little bold here. It's one thing to tell us how to *act*, but now he's telling us how to *think!*

He's right, though. The things you put into your mind will come out in your character. If you feed your mind with things that are pure and good, you'll have a healthy mind and a sound moral compass.

The most important way to do this is to read your Bible each morning so you'll have God's Word in your mind all day. You may want to read a chapter from the Gospels each day so that you're always learning from the life of Jesus. You might also want to read a chapter from Proverbs each day. (Since there are thirty-one, you can read one every day of the month.) You'll eventually want to read *every part* of the Bible so you can benefit from everything God has said.

Have you put some standards in place to make sure you don't let sin creep into your life through your mind? If you decide now what sort of movies you'll watch, what kind of books you'll read, what forms of music you'll listen to, and what type of humor you'll tolerate, it'll save you from getting caught off guard by temptation in the future.

So set your sights high for yourself. Decide today that you'll only allow into your mind things that are pleasing to Jesus.

WHAT STANDARDS ARE YOU PUTTING INTO PLACE TO KEEP SIN FROM CREEPING INTO YOUR MIND?

READ UP: 1 CHRONICLES 28:8–10 • MARK 12:28–34

I'M OKAY

READ AHEAD: PHILIPPIANS 4:10–11

I have learned to be content in whatever circumstances I am.
Philippians 4:11

There was a phrase floating around Christian circles a few years back on posters and bumper stickers: "A Christian is just one beggar telling another beggar where to find bread." Although this presents Christians as humble people (which we should be), this saying isn't totally accurate. Christians are *not* beggars! Christians are wealthy beyond description—wealthy in a way the world doesn't understand.

Paul at one time had been the epitome of success. He had climbed the ladder pretty well to the top. He was making a name for himself as a mover and shaker in the Jewish world. He had power, influence, and an impressive reputation.

Then he met Jesus, and his ambition did a complete about-face. Worldly success no longer meant anything to him. He was content whether he had a lot of money or no money, nice shelter or no shelter, good food or no food . . . because his contentment came from within.

Our society works hard to keep us discontent. We work harder and harder to get more and more—but it's still not enough. It's said that when Alexander the Great conquered the entire known world, he wept because there were no worlds left to conquer!

We need to learn that outward things will never be able to satisfy our inner longing for contentment. Only God can do that. So if you've been dissatisfied with your circumstances—before you ask God to change them, ask him to change your heart.

WHAT KEEPS YOU FROM BEING CONTENT?

READ UP: LUKE 12:13–21 • HEBREWS 13:5–6

EVERYTHING?

READ AHEAD: PHILIPPIANS 4:12–13

I am able to do all things through Him who strengthens me.
Philippians 4:13

A preschooler asked to do something that was beyond his capabilities. Fearing he would get hurt, his mother refused to let him do as he asked. With a scowl, her little son crossed his arms, stomped his foot, and said, "I can do all things through Christ, who strengthens me!"

Just like the little boy, we can easily become confused about God's promises. Paul never said we could decide to do anything we wanted to do and then force God to put his power behind our wishes.

But God does promise to carry out *his* desires through us. This means that whatever he asks us to do, we can do it—not because we're so extraordinarily gifted, but because he will give us the strength.

Bottom line? If you decide you want to be a millionaire, don't count on God to fulfill your desire. But if God has called you to do something, only one thing will prevent it from happening: your disobedience. If God wants to use your life to bring joy to a lonely person, or to teach a Bible study, or to be a missionary, the only thing standing in your way is your own unwillingness.

When God asks you to do something, don't waste your time deciding if it can be done. Just do it! Paul didn't say, "I am able do *some* things through Him who strengthens me." He said, "I can do *all things* through Him who strengthens me."

HOW HAVE YOU EXPERIENCED THIS KIND OF STRENGTHENING BEFORE?

READ UP: JUDGES 6:11–16 • MATTHEW 28:16–20

GOT'CHA COVERED

READ AHEAD: PHILIPPIANS 4:15–19

And my God will supply all your needs according to His riches in glory in Christ Jesus. Philippians 4:19

Christians can afford to be the most generous people in the world . . . because of the way God does the math.

God's math is different from ours. We think the more we give away, the less we have. But he says, "Go ahead and be generous, because the more you give away, the more I will give you."

Today's passage is a thank-you note from Paul to his friends in Philippi. They'd taken up a collection to help him continue serving as a missionary in another city. And as he commended them for their generosity, he also assured them that God would, in turn, be generous with them.

You can never outgive God. If you struggle to be generous with others, remember who's asking you to share your resources. When God asks you to give something away or to share what you have, don't worry that you'll come up short. He promises to take care of you, and his storehouse never gets empty.

If you're not already tithing, giving at least ten percent of your income to your church, make that a personal goal. Tithing is more about faith than it is about money. When you give the first portion of what you earn, you're showing God you trust him to take care of you. Christians talk a lot about God meeting our needs. We need to be sure we put our money where our mouth is.

WHY WOULD GOD INCLUDE GIVING AS SUCH AN IMPORTANT PART OF THE CHRISTIAN LIFE?

READ UP: MATTHEW 25:31–40 • 1 TIMOTHY 6:17–19

150

ANYTHING ELSE YOU
FEEL LIKE SAYING?

www.BroadmanHolman.com

Don't miss these other great resources for students.